# Flavors
# of
# Fredericksburg

**St. Barnabas Episcopal Church Women**
**Fredericksburg, Texas**

Cover Illustration: By Lee Ethel
*Two Ten West Travis* 1987
From the collection of Bob and Janice Phelps, New Orleans, Louisiana

## Lee Ethel

Lee Ethel was born in Hydro, Oklahoma and moved to Miami, Texas with his family at age 15. His artistic talent was discovered by a fifth grade teacher, and following high school he studied at Oklahoma A&M in Stillwater, the Los Angeles Art Center and Southern Methodist University in Dallas, Texas. He also studied under Margaret Leibold, Charles Lord Nelson, and David Hardy. Mr. Ethel utilized his artistic talent and training in a career as a graphic designer in the advertising industry, working primarily in the Dallas area. In the early 1970s Lee and his wife Betty, along with daughters Pam and Susan, discovered Fredericksburg on a return trip from South Padre Island. They bought the old Carl Henke home and in 1974 began restoration of it while Lee maintained his career in Dallas. He retired from commercial art in 1982. Lee then combined his artistic talent with a love for Americana and Texana to create a distinctive style of painting described as "bold, yet sensitive; vigorous, yet subtle." He exhibited his work in galleries in Texas, Arkansas, Oklahoma, and California. His pieces are included in corporate and private collections throughout the United States, Mexico and Europe.

Lee Ethel's talent and dedication have made a great impact on the Fredericksburg community, both in his church, St. Barnabas Episcopal, and on the lives of all who collect and admire his art.

*December 1, 1926–December 2, 1992*

Copyright © 1993
St. Barnabas Episcopal Church Women
Fredericksburg, Texas

First Printing, September, 1993
Second Printing, November, 1994
Third Printing, August, 2000

ISBN 0-9641687-0-7

**WIMMER**
The Wimmer Companies
Memphis

Printed in the USA by

# Acknowledgements

We are deeply grateful for the life of Lee Ethel. Through his brush and colorful palette, Lee captured the beauty and enchantment of Fredericksburg. We appreciate the generosity of Betty Ethel and all the owners of Lee's paintings in sharing his work with our cookbook and therefore with its readers.

A sincere thank you to all the cookbook committee and others who have given so much time and effort in collecting and testing all the recipes. This endeavor is our expression of our love and devotion to the glory of God.

*Alethia Alt*

## Cookbook Committee

| | | | |
|---|---|---|---|
| General Chairman: | Alethia Alt | Typists: | Bonnie Greene |
| | | | Sande Knapp |
| Recipes: | Alethia Alt | | Lee Ann Montandon |
| | Lauren Bade | | Nancy O'Neal |
| | Sarah Campbell | | Jan Peterson |
| | Ruth Holman | | Patti Richard |
| | Mary Lindsey | | Doris Smith |
| | Jeannine Miller | | Mary Ann Taylor |
| | Virginia Muncey | | Betty Robinson |
| | Nancy O'Neal | | |
| | Jan Peterson | Accountant: | George and Mary Ann Williamson |
| | Doris Smith | | |
| | Mary Ann Taylor | Art and Layout: | Martha Kipcak and Jan Peterson |
| | Mary Ann Williamson | | |
| | Linda Zehnder | Marketing: | Mary Lindsey and Linda Zehnder |

## Introduction

St. Barnabas Episcopal Mission was formed in Fredericksburg, Texas in 1952. The five original families met in their homes to worship for two years until they purchased the fachwerk cabin (as seen on the cover — left side) built by immigrant William Walter in 1848.

On St. Barnabas Day in 1964 ground was broken for a new sanctuary. President and Mrs. Johnson presented an ancient stone from the wall of the St. Barnabas Monastery in Cyprus, to be placed in the new structure.

The work of Lee Ethel is only one example of the fine artistic gifts of St. Barnabas parishioners. Exquisite needlepoint kneelers and the rich symbolism of our unique stained glass windows contribute to a worshipful atmosphere.

By the Grace of God, St. Barnabas will continue to make history as we grow in our love of God and our neighbors.

## Organization

The St. Barnabas Episcopal Church Women's organization is dedicated to mission, outreach, and the loving concern for each other.

The proceeds from this book will help to continue our work with battered women, the Community Needs Council, scholarships for the local Children's Chorale, Hospice, Gillespie County children's services, New Horizons, Literacy Council, and various needs of the parish and community.

# Table of Contents

## *FAIR PARADE* 1982

### From the collection of
### Jim and D'Metra Riggs, Fredericksburg, Texas

The Gillespie County Fair is the highlight of every August. Businesses close, traffic is rerouted and parties are held on the balconies of the main street buildings. The whole town turns out for the big event!

# Broiled Crab Crostini

8 oz. lump crabmeat
   or imitation
1/2 cup diced red bell
   pepper
2 Tbsp. plus 2 tsp.
   mayonnaise
2 Tbsp. chopped fresh
   parsley
1 Tbsp. chopped fresh
   chives
1 Tbsp. fresh lime
   juice
1 Tbsp. Dijon mustard
2 tsp. grated parmesan
4 or 5 drops hot
   pepper sauce
4 oz. of Italian bread
   thin sliced into
   16 slices
Rosemary, fresh
   chopped

Preheat broiler. Line broiler pan with foil. Pick any cartilage out of crabmeat. Combine all ingredients, except bread, in a bowl and mix well. Spread 1 Tbsp. of the mixture on each slice of bread. Place these on broiler pan and broil 4 or 5 inches from heat for 5 to 6 minutes, or until lightly brown. Sprinkle lightly with chopped rosemary.

*Danye Dolan Alt*

# Cheese Crisps

2 cups sharp cheddar
   (grated)
2 sticks margarine
2 cups flour
2 cups Rice Krispies
1/4 tsp. red pepper
1/2 tsp. salt

Soften margarine and mix with cheese. Add flour, pepper, salt and Rice Krispies. Mix thoroughly. Shape into 1 inch balls. Place on ungreased cookie sheet. Press with fork dipped in water. Bake at 350 degrees 18 to 20 minutes. Cool on brown paper sacks. Store in airtight container. Will keep for weeks.

*Nancy Kimbrell*

# Cheese Log

| | |
|---|---|
| 1/2 lb. sharp cheddar cheese, grated | 2 Tbsp. dill pickle relish |
| 2 Tbsp. minced onion | 1 Tbsp. chopped pimiento |
| 3 Tbsp. minced green pepper | 1 hard-boiled egg, chopped |
| | 1 cup crushed Ritz crackers |

Mix all together well, form into two logs. Wrap in waxed paper, and refrigerate until well chilled. Serve with assorted crackers.

*Gloria Jones*

# Cheese Straws

| | |
|---|---|
| 1 lb. sharp cheddar cheese, grated | 2 cups flour |
| 1 1/2 sticks margarine | 1/2 tsp. salt |
| | 3/4 tsp. red pepper |

Let cheese and margarine soften. Add flour, salt, and red pepper. Mix well. Press through cookie press using "star" plate. Cookie sheets can be lightly oiled. Bake at 300 degrees for 20 minutes. Let cool on cookie sheets for a few minutes, then transfer to paper towel.

*Kathleen Bridges*

# Crab Meat Mold

| | |
|---|---|
| 8 oz. softened cream cheese | 1 envelope unflavored gelatin, dissolved in 1/8 cup water |
| 1 small grated onion | 1/2 cup mayonnaise |
| 1/2 can cream of mushroom soup, undiluted | 1/2 cup chopped celery |
| | 1 1/2 cups canned crab meat |

Heat soup; stir in gelatin which has been dissolved in water and cream cheese. Beat until smooth. Add remaining ingredients and pour into small greased mold. Chill until firm. Serve with crackers.

*Ruby Edwards*

# Cream Cheese Dip

| | |
|---|---|
| 8 oz. NO FAT cream cheese (Healthy choice is good) | 1/4 tsp. garlic powder |
| | 1/4 tsp. cayenne pepper |
| | 1/4 tsp. of any 6 herbs |

Combine all ingredients. Refrigerate for at least 1 hour before serving to let flavors blend. Serve with crackers or toast rounds.

*NANA'S TEA ROOM, Fredericksburg*

# Cream Cheese Olives

1 large jar stuffed green olives
1 8 oz. pkg. cream cheese

Pecans, chopped very fine

Soften cream cheese with some salad dressing. Drain and dry olives. Roll olives in cream cheese mixture and then roll in nuts. Chill. Slice in half. Chill again and serve.

*Mary Ann Taylor*

# Cucumber Dip

1 8 oz. pkg. cream cheese (regular or low cal)
1 small onion, hand grated
1 to 3 cucumbers, peeled and hand grated

Salt
Pepper
Seasoned salt
Other seasoning to taste

Let cream cheese come to room temperature. Add other ingredients. I use this as a sandwich spread as well as a dip.

*C.C. Gibbons*

# Ernie's Deer Wraps

*(This recipe was given to us by our neighbor, Ernie Carlson, and it is the very best recipe, everyone loves it)*

Bacon cut into ¹/₂ strip
Jalapeño pepper, sliced
Deer meat cut into 1¹/₂"x1"x1" or small strips

MARINADE (for 50 wraps):
1 medium bottle worcestershire sauce
2 Tbsp. liquid smoke
2 Tbsp. garlic powder
3 tsp. celery powder

Using ROUND toothpicks, wrap 1 piece of meat around 1 slice jalapeño pepper. Wrap meat and pepper with ¹/₂ slice bacon. Skewer with toothpicks, soak in marinade overnight or several hours. Cook on grill (inside or outside) until done.

*Jim Smith*

# Fay's Armadillo Eggs

**24 pickled, whole jalapeño peppers, with stems**
**2 lbs. pork sausage**
**1 cup grated cheddar cheese**
**24 canned biscuits**

Split pepper, deseed, leaving stem on. Stuff with cheese, put halves back together. Cover stuffed pepper with sausage. Bake at 350 degrees, in pre-heated oven, until sausage is almost done, 6-7 minutes. Drain. Cool. Flatten biscuit and wrap around sausage. Bake at 350 degrees until brown, about 15-20 minutes.

*Fay Carlson*

# Guacamole

**2 ripe avocados**
**1 1/2 Tbsp. lime or lemon juice**
**1 large ripe tomato, chopped**
**2 Tbsp. finely chopped onion**
**1 crushed and finely chopped garlic clove**
**1 small green pepper finely chopped (optional)**

Peel and pit avocados, saving the pits. Mash with potato masher until chunky. Add remaining ingredients and mix thoroughly. You can omit the pepper and put some mild picante sauce in the mixture. Press the pits into mixture or put saran on surface to keep guacamole from browning. Refrigerate until ready to serve. Remove pits.

*Jeannine Miller*

*Try some lemon juice on cooked vegetables, meats or soups; it enhances their flavors.*

# La Fogata's Chilie Strips

6 poblano chilies,
   roasted and peeled
1 onion halved and cut
   in strips
2-3 Tbsp. vegetable oil
8 oz. cream cheese,
   cut in 4-5 pieces

$1/2$ tsp. garlic powder
Pinch of cumin
Salt to taste
6 oz. Oaxaca or
   mozzarella cheese,
   grated
6-8 hot flour tortillas

Stem and seed the chilies and cut into narrow strips. Sauté the onion in oil until soft and translucent, about 5-8 minutes. Do not brown. Add the chilies and cook 1 minute, then add the cream cheese and spices. When the cream cheese is completely melted, add the grated Oaxaca or mozzarella in 6-8 handfuls. Allow the cheese to melt without stirring and take care to keep the temperature low. Serve in individual ramekins with a hot flour tortilla draped over the top of each bowl. To eat, the raja mixture is simply spooned onto the tortilla, which is rolled or folded to keep the mixture from spilling out. Note: The chilie and onion mixture may be prepared up to 2 days in advance and either refrigerated or frozen until ready to use. Be sure to reheat it before adding the 2 cheeses. Serves 6-8.

*Martha Kipcak*

*Freeze chicken broth in 2-4 cup containers. They will defrost quickly, and may be used instead of water in cooking vegetables or soups.*

# Oyster Roll

2 cans smoked oysters, drained, rinsed and mashed
1 16 oz. package cream cheese

1/4 cup chopped onion
2 tsp. worcestershire sauce
1/2 cup mayonnaise

Mold in piece of waxed paper and roll in parsley and chopped pecans.

*Jeannine Miller*

# Pico De Gallo

2-3 fresh jalapeño peppers, minced
4-6 green onions, sliced (use all of white and most of green)
3-4 tomatoes, chopped

2 Tbsp. fresh cilantro or flakes
Juice of 1/2 lime
Sprinkle of garlic powder
Salt to taste

Mix all together and serve on fajitas or chips. Add more peppers if desired.

*Barbara Ann Pressler*

# Ruby's Hot Tamale Dip

1 can chili (about 15 oz.)
2 cans tamales, shucked and mashed

1/2 lb. cheddar cheese, grated
Cayenne pepper, salt and worcestershire sauce to taste

Cook in double boiler until cheese melts. Stir until thoroughly blended and heated. Serve in chafing dish to keep warm. Good with Fritos or tortilla chips.
Makes 1 1/2 qts.

*Mary Lindsey*

# Jalapeño Pie

1 11 oz. can jalapeños
1 cup grated cheddar cheese

1 cup grated monterey jack cheese
6 eggs

Lightly grease 13 1/2"x8 3/4" pan. Chop 3/4 cup jalapeños and distribute over bottom of pan. Mix grated cheeses and sprinkle over jalapeños. Beat eggs and pour evenly over cheese. Bake at 325 degrees for 25 minutes. Cut into small squares.

*Mary Lindsey*

# Salmon Spread

1 can red salmon,
   mashed and
   drained
1 8 oz. pkg. cream
   cheese
2 Tbsp. reserved
   salmon liquid

1 tsp. liquid smoke
1/4 cup grated onion
Minced garlic (about
   1/2 tsp.)
Lemon juice
Black pepper
Salt

Soften cream cheese, add rest of ingredients, and mix together well. Line with wax paper (or saran) with chopped parsley and chopped pecans, add salmon and roll into log shape on parsley mixture. Wrap and chill several hours. (You can put salmon mixture on decorative plate and put parsley/pecans on top.)

*Stella Hill*

*Add a cup or more of refried beans to thicken or spice up soup.*

# Somsee's Egg Rolls

3/4 lb. cooked ground
   beef or chopped
   chicken or fish
2 cups chopped
   cabbage
3 carrots cut fine or
   grated
1 cup onion, minced
Salt and pepper to taste
2 eggs

1 sm. pkg. (1.75 oz)
   chinese noodles
   (bean thread)
1 16 oz. egg roll
   wrappers
DIPPING SAUCE:
3 Tbsp. soy sauce
1 Tbsp. red wine
   vinegar
1 tsp. sugar

Soak noodles in enough water to cover. Drain and chop. Mix noodles in bowl with cabbage, carrots, and onions. Stir in meat and eggs. Place a Tbsp. of mixture in egg roll wrapper that has been lightly spread with a slightly beaten raw egg. Roll wrapper with ends tucked in. Fry with oil in Wok or heavy skillet until golden brown, turning once or twice. Serve with Dipping sauce made from soy sauce, red wine vinegar and sugar. Makes about 18 rolls. (To make spicier rolls add 2 tsp. soy sauce and garlic powder to taste.)

*Somsee Pornphet*

# Shrimp and Crab Hot Dip

1 1/4 sticks butter
8 Tbsp. flour
1 1/2 cups milk
2 cups chopped celery
1 bouillon cube
1/2 cup water
1 small jar chopped pimiento
1 small can sliced mushrooms
1 medium can button mushrooms
2 1/2 tsp. mei yen

2 tsp. fresh pepper
1 Tbsp. chopped parsley
3 Tbsp. grated onion
1 1/2 Tbsp. worcestershire sauce
Tabasco to taste
1 can fresh or frozen crab meat
Amount of shrimp desired, boiled and peeled

Melt 1 stick butter, add flour and milk to make a cream sauce. Sauté celery in 1/4 stick butter until celery is tender. Add bouillon made with bouillon cube and water. Add celery to cream sauce. Stir. Add remaining ingredients. Serve hot in chafing dish with toast rounds.

*Jan Peterson*

# Shrimp Dip

1 8 oz. pkg. cream cheese
1 cup Kraft Thousand Island Dressing
1/2 cup mayonnaise
1 cup chopped green onion

3 to 6 tsp. Tabasco
1 Tbsp. seasoned salt
1 Tbsp. horseradish
Diced pimiento
1 lb. cooked shrimp, chopped

Cream softened cheese with dressing and mayonnaise. Stir in remaining ingredients. Chill and serve with chips or crackers.

*Shirley Crooks*

# Shrimply Divine Dip

| | |
|---|---|
| 1 3 oz. pkg. cream cheese | 1⁵/₈ oz. pkg. Italian salad dressing mix |
| 1 cup sour cream | ¹/₂ cup cooked or canned shrimp chopped fine |
| 2 tsp. lemon juice | |

Blend all together. Refrigerate until served.

*Jeanine Smith*

*Stick four cloves in a small onion and add when cooking chicken broth; it gives it a delightful flavor.*

# Spinach Balls

| | |
|---|---|
| 2 boxes frozen chopped spinach, cooked and drained dry | 6 eggs, beaten |
| 1 small 8 oz. bag herb stuffing | ¹/₂ cup Parmesan cheese, grated |
| 2 large onions chopped fine | ¹/₂ tsp. black pepper |
| | 1 Tbsp. garlic salt |
| | ¹/₂ tsp. thyme |
| | ³/₄ cup butter, melted |

Mix together and shape into small balls. Place on cookie sheet. Freeze until solid. Put in bags in freezer. Defrost. Bake at 350 degrees for 20 minutes. Makes 100 small balls. Even spinach-haters love these. Great for Christmas, weddings and all large gatherings.

*Doris Smith and Doris Schmid*

# Spinach Pesto Cheesecake

| | |
|---|---|
| 3/4 cup fine dry breadcrumbs | 1/4 cup pinenuts or walnuts |
| 1/3 cup ground pinenuts or walnuts | 1 large clove garlic, cut in half |
| 1/4 cup grated parmesan cheese | 1/4 tsp. salt |
| 1/3 cup margarine, melted | 1/4 tsp. freshly ground pepper |
| 1 cup coarsely chopped fresh spinach | 1/3 cup olive oil |
| 1/3 cup grated parmesan cheese | 3 8 oz. pkgs. cream cheese (non-fat works fine) |
| | 3 eggs |
| | 1/4 cup milk |

Combine first 4 ingredients, press on bottom and up sides of 8" springform pan. Process spinach and next 5 ingredients in food processor until smooth. With processor running, pour oil through chute in a steady stream until well blended. Beat cream cheese at high speed in mixer until fluffy. Add eggs one at a time beating after each addition. Add milk and spinach mixture. Pour mixture into prepared pan. Bake at 350 degrees for 1 hour. Turn oven off and partially open door, leave cheesecake in oven 1 hour. Chill. Garnish and serve with crackers.

# Tortilla Roll-Ups

| | |
|---|---|
| 12 burrito flour tortillas | Juice of one lime |
| 3 8 oz. pkgs. cream cheese | 1 Tbsp. picante sauce |
| 1 1/2 cup sour cream | 2 Tbsp. chopped cilantro |
| 1 bunch green onions with tops (chopped) | 4-6 slices pickled jalapeños (chopped) |

Mix all ingredients, except tortillas, together until smooth. Spread on tortillas and roll-up. Wrap in waxed paper and refrigerate. Allow to "set-up" at least 48 hours. Will keep for 10 days. Slice 1/2 inch thick. Serve with picante sauce.

*Ann Baker*

# FOURTH OF JULY AT THE GIBBONS 1991

## From the collection of
## George and C.C. Gibbons, Fredericksburg, Texas

Each year George and C.C. Gibbons, along with son George and his wife Lynn, pull out all the stops and throw a glorious Texas-size celebration of our nation's independence. Lee, as a faithful attendant of these extravaganzas, captured the fun and the spirit of this annual affair.

# Beef And Barley Soup

4 or 5 lbs. beef (or lamb with bones) use neck, shank or other cheap cuts
1 1/2 cup chopped onion
3-4 cloves garlic, minced
1/2 cup chopped celery with leaves
1/4 cup chopped parsley

3-4 large carrots chopped
1/2 Tbsp. thyme
1 large bay leaf
3/4 cup pearl barley
1 can tomatoes, sliced, 15 oz.
1 cup sliced carrots
1 cup chopped celery
1/2 cup chopped onion

In heavy bottom pot (6-8 qt.) put meat and bones that has all fat possible removed, 1 1/2 cup onion and 2 Tbsp. vegetable oil. Brown well. Add garlic, celery, parsley, carrots, thyme, and bay leaf. Cover with water, bring to boil, reduce heat and simmer 1 to 1 1/2 hours, skimming from time to time to remove froth and fat. Add water as needed. When meat is tender, let cool, preferably overnight in refrigerator for easy removal of fat. After fat is skimmed strain broth through a colander into another pot. Remove bones from meat. Discard bones and vegetables. An hour or so before serving add to broth the barley, tomatoes, 1 cup sliced carrots, celery and 1/2 cup onion. Cook until barley is tender. Return meat to broth, add salt & pepper to taste. Pour into large tureen, top with generous sprinkle of fresh chopped parsley. Serve with tossed green salad, crusty French bread and a bottle of modest red wine makes this an eminently soul-warming meal.

*John Schrenkeisen*

*French cooks say: Always keep a boiled chicken in your refrigerator. Then you are prepared for any quick meal or unexpected company.*

# Caldo Tlalpeno

4 cups chicken broth
2 chicken breasts
    halved, bone in,
    skinless
1/2 cup chopped celery
1/2 cup chopped onion
1/2 cup chopped carrot
Pinch of thyme
3-4 sprigs cilantro
1 lime or lemon
2 avocados, peeled and
    sliced right before
    serving
1 seeded jalapeño
    (more or less to
    taste), minced

Cook breasts in broth with celery, onion, carrot, and thyme, simmering gently about 40 minutes. Take breasts from pot and remove bone. Strain broth back into pot, add cilantro, chopped jalapeño, and salt to taste. Cook a few minutes, and add chicken. Before serving put sliced avocado (1/2 per person) and a sprinkle of crushed red pepper in each bowl and fill with hot soup. Serve with wedge of lime or lemon. This makes a great meal served with French bread and a salad or ripe tomatoes, fresh basil and feta cheese.

*John Schrenkeisen*

# Cheese, Potato And Wild Rice Soup

*(Quick and Easy!)*

1/2 cup wild rice,
    uncooked
1 1/2 cups water
1/2 lb. bacon, cut into
    pieces
1/4 cup chopped onion
2 10 3/4 oz. cans cream
    of potato soup
1 quart milk
2 1/2 cups grated
    American cheese
Carrot curls (optional)
    looks pretty on
    bowl of soup

Dilute potato soup with 2/3 cup milk and 2/3 cup water. Combine wild rice and water in saucepan and cook over low heat for 45 minutes. Drain. Set aside. Fry bacon pieces and onion in skillet until bacon is crisp. Drain bacon and onion on paper towel. Place ingredients with the rice in saucepan. Add cheese. Stir until cheese is melted. Serves 8.

*Jim Smith*

# Chilled Squash Soup with Mint

1 cup canned chicken broth
3 cups well-cooked squash (drained and pressed clear of liquid)
2 cups low fat yogurt
8 sprigs fresh mint, minced
Salt and pepper to taste

Mince squash in blender. Stir broth and squash together. Add yogurt and half the mint. Chill. Add remaining mint just before serving. It is better the second day. Serves 4.

*James Muncey*

*As my mother used to say: If there's enough, put a crust on it; if not, put it into a soup.*

# Chilled Tomato Soup

1/4 cup vegetable oil
2 cups chopped onion
3/4 cup chopped carrots
1 Tbsp. minced garlic
1 tsp. salt
1/2 tsp. cayenne pepper
4 cups chicken stock
4 lbs. tomatoes peeled, seeded and chopped
1/2 cup green onion, chopped
2 very ripe avocados
2/3 cup non-fat yogurt

Cook onion, carrots, and garlic in oil in 5 quart pan over medium heat. When vegetables are soft mix in salt and cayenne. Add stock and simmer partially covered 30 minutes. Increase heat, add tomatoes, and cook about 10 minutes. Cool slightly and purée in blender or processor. Cover and chill. In small bowl thoroughly blend avocados and yogurt. Serve in chilled bowls with a dollop of avocado cream. Sprinkle with green onions. Serves 6

*Linda Zehnder*

# Cold Cucumber Soup

| | |
|---|---|
| 2 large cucumbers, peeled and diced | 1 can chicken broth |
| 2 Tbsp. olive oil | 1/4 tsp. white pepper |
| 1 Tbsp. dill seed | 1 8 oz. carton plain yogurt |
| 1/3 cup finely diced onion | 1 8 oz. carton sour cream |
| 1 garlic clove, pressed | 1/4 cup chopped lightly toasted walnuts |
| 1 tsp. salt | |

Combine cucumber, olive oil, dill, garlic, salt, chicken broth, and white pepper. Let stand 3 hours. Purée 1/2 of mixture and add to chunky mixture. Stir in yogurt, sour cream, and walnuts. Chill for 8 hours before serving.

*Janice McDaniel*

# Cream of Broccoli and Cheese Soup

*(Microwave)*

| | |
|---|---|
| 2 cups chopped celery | 1 cup finely chopped onion |
| 1 10 oz. package chopped broccoli | 1 cup cottage cheese |
| 2 cups whole milk | 1 10³/₄ oz. can cream of chicken soup undiluted. |
| 1/2 tsp. salt, if desired | |
| 1/8 tsp. white pepper | |

Cook celery, onion and broccoli in 2¹/₂ quart covered casserole in microwave on HI for 6 minutes, stirring after 3 minutes. Set aside. Blend cottage cheese in blender until smooth, slowly add milk while blending. Add chicken soup to cheese/milk mixture then blend. Add mixture to cooked undrained vegetables. Microwave on high until heated through. Serve.

*Doris Smith*

*If your mother always cut a ham in half before she baked it, it may be because she didn't have a bigger pan.*

# Creamy Asparagus Soup

1 16 oz. can cut
   asparagus with
   liquid
1 cup cooked rice
$^1/_4$ cup chopped onion
$^1/_4$ cup chopped celery

$1^1/_2$ cups skimmed
   milk
Freshly ground black
   pepper
Dash nutmeg

Place canned asparagus and liquid in a blender with onion, celery, and cooked rice. Blend on low speed until puréed. Pour into a saucepan. Stir in milk. Season and heat to boiling point. Serve immediately. Yield: about $1^1/_4$ quarts.

*Billie Shingleton*

*An old Greek saying: A mother, while cooking, should never refuse her son if he asks for a bite or sample. This will insure he will not be impotent.*

# Egg-Lemon Soup

*This elegant Greek soup is an excellent first course or a main dish when pieces of cooked chicken are added.*

6 cups strong chicken
   stock
$^1/_2$ cup rice
1 tsp. flour

$^1/_4$ cup water
3 eggs
Juice of 2 large
   lemons

Bring stock to boil, salt to taste, add rice. Cover and boil gently 18 minutes. Measure out 3 cups stock into small saucepan. Cover remaining stock to keep hot. Make paste with flour and water, stir into the 3 cups of stock and boil gently 5 minutes. In a large bowl beat eggs with electric beater until thick and light in color. Add to eggs, by large spoonfuls, the boiling stock and the lemon juice, alternately, while continuing to beat. When all is mixed stir into pot of hot rice and stock. The soup should be frothy. Do not cover or cook or it will curdle. Serve immediately.

*Alethia Alt*

# Episcopal Soup

*(For A Large Family On A Cold Day)*

| | |
|---|---|
| 1 large soup bone | 1 cup diced turnips, (optional) |
| 1 lb. stew beef | 2 cups diced carrots |
| 3 qts. water | 1 cup diced celery |
| 2 large cans tomatoes | 1 cup chopped fresh |
| 2 large onions chopped | parsley (or 1/2 cup dried) |
| 2 thin slices of lemon | 1 can shoe peg corn |
| 1 red pepper pod | 1 can butter beans |
| 1/4 cup barley | 3 or 4 garlic cloves (optional) |
| Salt and pepper | |

Simmer soup bone and stew meat in 3 qts. water for 2 hours. Skim off fat. Add tomatoes, onion, lemon, red pepper, garlic, and barley. Salt and pepper to taste. Add carrots, celery, and parsley. Cook 1 1/2 hours, adding corn and beans the last 15 minutes. Remove soup bone. Serves 12-15.

*Vera Diaz*

# French Onion Soup

| | |
|---|---|
| 4 large onions, thinly sliced | 8 cups of strong beef broth |
| | 4 Tbsp. butter |
| | 1/4 tsp. thyme |
| | Salt and pepper to taste |

Melt butter in heavy saucepan with tight cover. Add onions and cover tightly. Steam over low heat for 25 minutes until tender. Combine the onions and their juices with the broth and simmer for 20 minutes. Serve with fresh grated parmesan cheese. Serves 5-6. Good with thinly sliced French bread floated on top.

*Jean W. Fourrier*

# French-Style Chicken Soup

2 cups cooked boned
   chicken, diced
   large
8 cups strong chicken
   broth
$^1/_3$ cup uncooked rice
$^1/_2$ cup frozen peas
1 cup celery, cut
   diagonally in 1 inch
   slices
1 cup chopped green
   onions with tops

$^1/_2$ cup dry white wine
$^3/_4$ tsp. dried thyme
$^1/_4$ tsp. savory or
   oregano
1 cup drained canned
   asparagus or sliced
   fresh zucchini
1 tsp. snipped parsley
$^1/_8$ tsp. pepper
$^1/_8$ tsp. garlic powder
Salt and pepper to
   taste

Combine chicken, rice, peas, celery, onions, wine, thyme, savory, garlic, and broth in soup pot. Bring to boil, reduce heat and simmer 15-20 minutes. Add asparagus and parsley and cook 5 more minutes. Add salt and pepper. Serves 10- 12.

*Barbara Smith*

# Green Chilies Cheese Soup

$^1/_2$ cup chopped onion
1 or 2 cloves garlic,
   minced
$^1/_4$ cup butter or
   margarine
$^1/_4$ cup flour
$^1/_2$ Tbsp. salt
$^1/_8$ Tbsp. pepper

3 cups milk (or 2%
   milk)
1 cup chicken broth
$^1/_4$ cup chopped green
   chilies
$1^1/_2$ cups shredded
   monterey jack
   cheese

Cook chopped onion and garlic in butter until tender. Stir in flour, salt and pepper. Add milk and broth. Stir over heat until slightly thickened and bubbly. Cook and stir one minute. Stir in peppers and cheese. Cook over low heat until cheese melts. For a really creamy soup run all through the blender. Add cumin and serve. Serves 6.

*Jan Fritz*

# Lentil Soup with Sausage

| | |
|---|---|
| 12 oz. package lentils | 2 cloves garlic, minced |
| 2 quarts water | 2 Tbsp. olive oil |
| 3 Tbsp. cocoa | 1/4 tsp. pepper |
| 1 1/2 oz. envelope onion soup mix | 1 bay leaf |
| 1 cup chopped celery | 1/2 lb. smoked sausage, sliced |
| 1 cup diced carrots | 1/4 cup Sherry wine |
| 2 lemon slices | |

In soup pot combine all ingredients except sausage and wine. Bring to boil. Simmer covered for 1 hour. Add sausage and wine. Cook 15 minutes uncovered. Season with salt. Garnish each bowl with thin lemon slice. Makes 6 (1 1/2 cup) servings.

*James Muncey*

# Mama's Oxtail Vegetable Soup

| | |
|---|---|
| 2 lbs. short ribs or oxtails | 1 can tomatoes |
| 2 Tbsp. salt | 3 stalks celery |
| 2 Tbsp. garlic salt | 1 cup cabbage, chopped |
| 2 tsp. celery salt | 2 large carrots |
| 1 bay leaf | Optional: a small amount of rice or noodles |
| 2 whole cloves | |
| 1/2 tsp. pepper | |
| 1 large onion | |

In large pot, cover meat with cold water. Add seasonings and cook until it falls from the bones (1 1/2 - 2 hours). Remove fat and bones. Cut meat in small pieces. If available, add chicken stock. Cut up and add: carrots, onion, tomatoes, celery, and cabbage. Add rice, if desired. Simmer until vegetables are just tender. Refrigerate and skim fat. Reheat before serving.

*Pat Reese*

# Senegalese Soup

1/4 cup olive oil
2 carrots, diced
3 celery stalks, diced
1/4 cup onion, chopped
1 1/2 Tbs. flour
2 tsp. curry powder (or more to taste)
4 cups chicken broth

1/3 cup apple, peeled and chopped fine
1 cup cooked chicken, minced
1/2 tsp. salt
1/4 tsp. pepper
1/8 tsp. thyme
1/3 cup shredded coconut
1/2 cup hot cream

Sauté carrots, celery and onion in oil until soft. Stir in flour and curry powder, stir for 1 minute. Slowly add chicken broth, stirring until smooth. Simmer for 30 minutes. Add apple, chicken, seasonings and coconut. Simmer for 15 minutes. Just before serving, stir in hot cream. Exotic and savory.

*Deborah Edwards*

# Tortilla Soup

10 cups strong chicken broth
2 cups diced onion
1/4 cup oil
6 cloves garlic
2 cups cooked chicken
2 tsp. ground cumin
1 can Rotel tomatoes with green chilies

1 15 oz. can stewed tomatoes
1 1/2 tsp. salt
1/2 cup chopped cilantro (optional)
1/4 cup grated cheese per bowl
Tostados or corn chips

In large pot sauté onion and garlic in oil until soft. Add the broth and other ingredients except cheese, bring to boil and simmer at least 30 minutes. Before filling bowls put in a few pieces of broken tostados or corn chips. Top with cheese. Serves 12 to 14.

*Elena Miller*

# Zucchini Soup

**4 cups strong defatted chicken broth, (or 7 bouillon cubes in 4 cups water)**
**6 zucchini, sliced**
**2 carrots, sliced**

**1/2 onion, sliced**
**8 ounces cream cheese, cubed**
**Salt and pepper to taste**
**4-5 dashes hot sauce**

Bring broth to boil. Add vegetables and simmer until they are tender. Purée in blender. Return to low heat and add cream cheese, season to taste. This is also good cold: (yogurt may be substituted for cream cheese when served cold). Allow vegetables to cool, add yogurt, blend, chill. Serves 6.

*Linda Zehnder*

*Freeze leftover soup in soup bowls; when frozen, dislodge soup, seal in plastic bags and store in freezer. Defrost as needed.*

# Antipasto Salad

1 package Rotini
  twirls pasta
1 1/4 cup cubed salami
  or ham
1 1/2 cup cubed
  provolone cheese
1 1/2 cup cherry
  tomatoes, halved
3/4 cup pitted black
  olives, sliced or
  whole

3/4 cup green pepper
  strips
1 jar sliced pimiento,
  drained
1 can baby corn,
  drained
1 jar artichoke hearts
1 or 2 carrots, sliced
  into fine sticks
1 bottle Italian
  dressing or
  homemade

Cook pasta; drain. Rinse with cold water to cool. In large bowl toss pasta with remaining ingredients until well blended. Chill, stirring occasionally.

Note: use any vegetables that you like to vary. This is great for crowds.

*Jeannine Miller*

# Avocado Bacon Salad

Juice of 2 limes
1/4 cup vegetable oil
1/2 cup sour cream
1/4 cup mayonnaise
2 cloves garlic,
  pressed

8 strips bacon, fried
  and crumbled
1 head lettuce, washed
  and torn into bite-
  sized pieces
2 small avocados,
  cubed
Salt and pepper

Combine first 6 ingredients for dressing. Cook bacon, drain and crumble. Combine at serving time the lettuce, avocado, and bacon. Toss gently with dressing. Tomato wedges are a nice addition or garnish to this salad.

*David Smith*

# Avocado Mushroom Piquant

| | |
|---|---|
| 1/2 cup salad oil | 3/4 tsp. salt |
| 3 Tbsp. tarragon vinegar | 3 avocados, peeled, pitted, and sliced |
| 2 Tbsp. lemon juice | 8 oz. fresh mushrooms, halved lengthwise (3 cups) |
| 2 Tbsp. water | Dash pepper |
| 1 Tbsp. snipped parsley | Parsley sprigs |
| 1 clove garlic, minced | |

In screw-top jar combine oil, vinegar, lemon juice, water, snipped parsley, garlic, salt, and pepper. Cover and shake to blend. Pour over avocados and mushrooms in a shallow dish. Chill several hours, spooning marinade over occasionally. To serve, drain avocados and mushrooms; arrange vegetables on platter. Garnish with parsley sprigs. Makes 8 servings.

*Gretchen McWilliams*

# Black Bean Salad

| | |
|---|---|
| 2 15 oz. cans black beans, drained and rinsed | 2 Tbsp. fresh cilantro, chopped |
| 1 cup chopped tomatoes | 1/2 purple onion, chopped |
| 1 large sweet red pepper, chopped | 1 envelope (0.7 oz) Italian dressing mix |
| 2/3 cup sliced green onions | 1/2 cup water 1/4 cup red wine vinegar |
| 1/2 cup celery, chopped | 2 tbs. olive oil |
| 1 clove garlic, minced | 1/4 tsp. cumin (cominos) to taste |

Combine the first 8 ingredients and set aside. Combine dressing mix with remaining ingredients in a jar and shake vigorously. Pour dressing over salad and toss gently. Cover and chill. Toss again before serving. Serves 8. Only 140 calories per 3/4 cup serving!

*Karen Laurence*

# Caesar Salad

1 clove garlic
1/4 cup olive oil
2 cups of 1/4" fresh
 bread cubes
2 heads romaine
 lettuce
1/4 cup grated fresh
 Parmesan cheese
1/4 cup crumbled blue
 cheese
1/2 cup olive oil

1 Tbsp. worcestershire
 sauce
3/4 tsp. salt
1/4 tsp. freshly ground
 black pepper
1/4 cup fresh lemon
 juice
1 egg (optional)
2" tube anchovy paste
 (optional)

Early in day: quarter garlic; drop into 1/4 cup olive oil and set aside. Toast bread squares in shallow pan at 300 degrees for 20 minutes or until golden. Put lettuce that has been torn into bite size into a salad bowl. Refrigerate.

Just before serving sprinkle greens with cheese and drizzle over top the 1/2 cup olive oil mixed with worcestershire, anchovy paste, salt and pepper. Toss gently until every leaf glistens. Break whole raw egg onto greens; pour lemon juice over all; toss until egg specks disappear. Now pour the 1/4 cup olive oil (remove the garlic first) over the bread squares, toss and sprinkle over greens. Toss salad, serve at once. Serves 6.

*Dr. Charles Schmidt*

*Mother used to say to never drink water after eating pickled or fried fish because your mouth will taste like live fish are swimming around in it. Eat some other food before you drink.*

# Curried Rice Salad

| 1 1/2 cup cooked rice | 1/2 tsp. curry powder |
| 1/4 cup minced onions | 1 tsp. salt |
| 1 Tbsp. vinegar 2 |
| Tbsp. salad oil |

Mix together above ingredients and refrigerate 3 hours. Add:

| 1 cup diced celery | 1/2 cup mayonnaise to |
| 1 8 oz. pkg. frozen | taste |
| green peas, |
| uncooked |

Add more salt if needed. Mix well and chill before serving.

*Anita Page*

# Dreamy Apricot Salad

| 1 8 oz. package | 2 3 oz. packages |
| softened cream | apricot gelatin |
| cheese | 2/3 cup sugar |
| 1 can sweetened | 2 4 3/4 oz. jar apricot |
| condensed milk | baby food |
| 1 cup chopped pecans | 1 20 oz. can crushed |
| | pineapple |

Combine gelatin, sugar and 2/3 cup of water in a saucepan. Bring to a boil, stirring to dissolve gelatin and sugar, then remove from heat and add fruit. Cool. Beat cream cheese and condensed milk in bowl until smooth. Combine with gelatin mixture and pecans mixing well. Pour into a 2 quart mold or dish. Chill until firm. Unmold on serving dish. Serves 16.

*Billie Shingleton*

*To peel peaches or tomatoes easily, drop them in boiling water for a few minutes. The skins will slip off easily.*

# Marinated Vegetable Salad

10 oz. of canned or homemade chicken broth
1 or 2 bay leaves
$1/2$ to 1 tsp. salt
Black pepper to taste
1 package frozen baby lima beans
1 or 2 cups carrots, sliced diagonally
$1/4$ lb. small white onions or 1 or 2 bunches green onions
1 can small peas
1 can green beans
$1/2$ cup sliced celery
MARINADE:
$1/2$ cup lemon juice
$1/4$ cup salad oil
1 tsp. brown sugar
$1/2$ tsp. dry mustard
$1/2$ tsp. garlic salt or 1 clove, pressed

Cook broth and seasonings 5 minutes. Add baby lima beans, carrots and onions. Cook 8 minutes. Drain all vegetables and marinate in oil mixture for several hours or overnight. Broth mixture may be saved for other cooking.

*Florence Young*

# Mexican Salad

6 large lettuce leaves
2-3 cups shredded head lettuce
2 medium tomatoes, chopped
$1/2$ cup onion, chopped
$1^1/3$ cups slightly crushed tostado chips
$1^1/3$ cups Ranch Style beans with juice, heated
1 cup grated cheddar cheese
6-8 jalapeño slices
2 heaping Tbsp. guacamole
2 Tbsp. sliced black olives(optional)
Nacho chips
Picante sauce
$1/2$ cup oil and vinegar dressing
Salt and pepper to taste

Line two large salad bowls (8 inch) with lettuce leaves. In each bowl put half the shredded lettuce, chopped tomatoes, onions, crushed chips, and hot beans with juice. Top with cheese, olives and jalapeños. Pour $1/4$ cup dressing on each. Put guacamole in center. Place nacho chips around inside edge of bowls. Serve picante sauce in side dish.

*ALTDORF BIERGARTEN, Fredericksburg*

# Monterey Salad And Dressing

1/2 head washed, dried,
picked leaf lettuce
1 peeled and julienned
Jicama
2 cups washed, picked
fresh spinach
1 cup chopped red
cabbage
1 red onion sliced in
rings
2 thinly sliced
radishes

**DRESSING:**
3/4 cup unsweetened
frozen orange juice
concentrate
3 Tbsp. balsamic
vinegar
3 Tbsp. canola oil
1/4 tsp. dry mustard
Black pepper and salt
to taste.

1 orange peeled and
sectioned

Mix orange juice and vinegar. Whisk in oil and seasonings. Arrange vegetables and oranges on platter.
Spoon dressing over salad. Serves 8.

*Billie Shingleton*

# Pressler Potato Salad

4 lbs. potatoes, peeled,
cut in chunks
1 cup sliced green
onions
1 cup real mayonnaise

1 Tbsp. prepared
horseradish
1 Tbsp. cider vinegar
1 1/2 tsp. salt
1 tsp. sugar
1/2 tsp. pepper

Boil potatoes until tender, but firm. Drain. Add onions. Mix all other ingredients for a dressing. Whisk
together and pour over potatoes. Mix well and chill.
Serve on bed of lettuce. Makes 8 cups. Calories: 160
per 1/2 cup. Serves 16.

*Barbara Ann Pressler*

*"An apple a day keeps the doctor away" is not a
joke — it really is the truth.*

# The Real Greek Salad

4 large firm ripe
tomatoes
1¹/₂ cups sliced
cucumbers (remove
seeds)
1 cup or more chopped
green onions, with
tops
2 stalks of celery,
chopped

1 medium zucchini,
chopped
1 Tbsp. oregano
2 or 3 garlic cloves,
peeled
Salt and pepper
¹/₂ cup feta cheese,
crumbled
¹/₂ cup olive oil
¹/₄ cup lemon juice or
wine vinegar

In a wooden salad bowl mash and rub garlic cloves all around. Add tomatoes cut in wedges, cucumbers, onions, celery and zucchini. Salt and pepper to taste. Sprinkle with oregano, crushing it between your fingers as you do. Mix oil and lemon juice (if using vinegar, add a pinch of sugar). Pour over salad and toss it well. Top with feta and serve on romaine leaves. Serves 8.

*Alethia Alt*

# Red Cabbage Salad

1 head red cabbage,
chopped
1 bunch red grapes,
seedless, sliced

1 avocado, sliced
1 6 or 8 oz. bottle
poppy seed
dressing.

Combine all ingredients and add poppy seed dressing.

*Doris Smith*

# Spinach Salad And Dressing

1 lb. raw spinach
1¹/₂ cup chopped
green onion
5 hard boiled eggs,
chopped
5 slices bacon

DRESSING:
¹/₂ cup oil
¹/₂ cup vinegar
¹/₂ cup sugar
1 tsp. salt

Fry bacon crisp, drain and crumble. Rinse spinach well, drain and chop. Combine in salad bowl: bacon, spinach, onions and eggs. Dressing: Mix well the ingredients for dressing and pour over salad. Toss together.

*Sandie Smallwood*

# Shell Pasta Salad

**1 pkg. large shell pasta**
**1 cup green olives coarsely chopped**
**1/2 cup green peas**
**4 green onions chopped**
**1/2 cup celery finely chopped**
**Mayonnaise**

Cook pasta, drain, cool quickly with cold water. Add all ingredients and moisten with mayonnaise. Best if chilled several hours or overnight.

*Jeannine Miller*

# Shrimp Salad Mold

**1 can tomato soup**
**1 pkg. unflavored gelatin**
**1/4 cup water**
**1 8 oz. pkg. cream cheese**
**1/2 cup chopped green pepper**
**1/2 cup celery, chopped**
**1/2 cup onion, chopped**
**2 lb. cleaned, boiled shrimp, small or chopped medium**
**1 cup mayonnaise**
**Tabasco and/or horseradish to taste (optional)**

Heat soup to boiling, add gelatin dissolved in water. Add cheese. Beat until smooth with rotary beater or wire whisk. Add mayonnaise and mix well. Pour over chopped vegetables and shrimp and mix. Chill in 1 1"x7" casserole or in ring mold, or in individual molds. Great at luncheons! Serves 4-6.

*Jeannine Miller*

# Sour Cream Cucumbers

1/2 tsp. salt
1 Tbsp. sugar
2 Tbsp. cider vinegar
1 cup sour cream
2 Tbsp. chives,
  chopped
2 Tbsp. fresh dill,
  chopped
1 tsp. celery seed
2 firm cucumbers,
  unpeeled

Dissolve salt and sugar in vinegar, add sour cream and stir until smooth. Add chives, dill and celery seed. Slice cucumbers paper thin and combine with dressing. Chill 1 hour or more.

*Doris Smith*

# Vegetable Coleslaw

4 cups shredded
  cabbage
2 medium-sized
  zucchini, diced
2 medium-sized
  summer squash,
  diced
1 bunch green onions,
  chopped
1 cup light
  mayonnaise
1/2 cup cider vinegar
1 Tbsp. mustard seed
1/2 tsp. celery salt

Combine the cabbage, zucchini, squash and onions. Combine the mayonnaise, vinegar, mustard seed and celery salt. Add the mayonnaise mixture to the cabbage mixture and toss to coat. Refrigerate at least 4 hours. Serves 8.

*Doris Smith*

*Whether you store cheese in or out of the refrigerator; to keep it fresh, cover it with a cloth moistened with vinegar.*

# Willa Marie's Green Bean Salad

2 cans (16 oz.) whole green beans
1 bunch green onions, chopped
1 can mushrooms, drained and chopped
1 can water chestnuts, drained
1 small bottle stuffed green olives, sliced
1 can sliced artichoke hearts, drained
2 Tbsp. olive oil
1 Tbsp. parsley flakes
1 Tbsp. oregano
Juice of 2 lemons
Garlic salt to taste

Combine all ingredients and marinate in refrigerator at least 6 hours. Serves 6 or 8.

*Willa Marie Dietz*

# Yum Yum Salad

2 cups crushed pineapple
1 lemon, juice only
1 cup sugar
2 Tbsp. gelatin
1/2 cup cold water
1 cup grated American cheese
1/2 pt. whipped cream (not sweetened)

Heat pineapple. Add lemon juice and sugar. Stir until sugar is dissolved. Soak gelatin in cold water for 10 minutes. Add to hot mixture. When cool and beginning to set, add cheese and whipped cream. Mix thoroughly and freeze. Serve after thawing slightly. Serves 8-10.

*Nell Simes*

*SUNDAY AFTERNOON*                                    1992

From the collection of
Betty Ethel, Fredericksburg, Texas

Lee's last work is a rendition of a quiet Sunday afternoon in Fredericksburg. Shown are some of the historical landmarks: the library, gazebo, Vereins Kirche, Marien Kirche, White Elephant Saloon, Nimitz Museum, Tatsch House, Pioneer Museum, St. Barnabas Chapel, peach groves and Cross Mountain.

# Baked Spaghetti Casserole

1 1/2 lbs. thin spaghetti
2 lbs. ground beef
2 Tbsp. olive oil
1 cup chopped onion
5 cloves garlic, peeled and pressed
2 6 oz. cans tomato paste
2 15 oz. cans tomato sauce (or 1 can sauce and 1 can chopped tomatoes)
4 cups water
1/2 cup red wine
1 cup sour cream or half and half
1 Tbsp. dried oregano,
2 tsp. dried basil
2 tsp. salt
1/2 tsp. pepper
1 cup grated parmesan
1 cup grated mozzarella

Bring 7 qts. water to boil for pasta. While this is heating, cook meat in a heavy pot (4 qts.) stirring often until brown. Drain. Add to meat: olive oil, chopped onion and garlic. Sauté a minute or so then add tomato paste, tomato sauce, water, wine, sour cream, basil, oregano, salt and pepper. Simmer 20 minutes. Cook spaghetti in boiling water until barely tender (al dente). Drain pasta, add meat sauce to pasta and mix. Put 1/3 of the pasta and meat mixture in a 16"x11"x3" baking pan (a turkey roaster will do). Sprinkle with 1/3 cup of each cheese, make 2 more layers of pasta and cheeses. Bake uncovered at 350 degrees for 25 minutes or until all is bubbly hot. This can be assembled the day before. Cover and refrigerate until ready to bake and serve. Serves 20.

*Christina Straka*

# Beef & Fresh Greens Salad With Raspberry Lemon Vinaigrette

1 head each red leaf
lettuce, Boston
lettuce, chickory
lettuce, watercress
1 bunch watercress
1 lb. beef flank steak
(or left over beef)
4 green onions, sliced
in 1/4 inch pieces
1/2 yellow pepper,
diced
1/4 cup chopped
walnuts
DRESSING:
5 oz. frozen
raspberries in syrup

1/2 cup cilantro leaves
1 inch piece ginger
root, peeled
Juice and grated rind
of 1 lemon
1/2 tsp. salt
1/4 cup balsamic
vinegar
1/3 cup canola or light
salad oil
Garnish: yellow and
red bell peppers
slices, asparagus
tips and fresh
raspberries

Arrange greens decoratively on salad plates. To prepare dressing blend all ingredients except oil in food
processor or blender while slowly adding oil. Broil
steak to medium. Slice across the grain at an angle
to make slices wider than the thickness of the steak.
Toss with 1/2 cup of the dressing and remaining
ingredients except garnish. Divide beef mixture and
place equal portions on each plate of greens. Garnish with peppers, asparagus and raspberries, if
desired. Serves 4.

*Diane Matthews*

# Chili Queen Chili

2 lbs. beef shoulder
(cut in 1/2" cubes)
1 lb. pork shoulder
(cut in 1/2" cubes)
3 medium sized
onions, chopped
6 garlic cloves,
chopped
1 qt. water

4 ancho chilies
1 serrano chilie
6 dried red chilies
1 Tbsp. comino seeds
(freshly ground)
2 Tbsp. Mexican
oregano
Salt to taste

Place lightly floured beef and pork cubes in oil in heavy chili pot and cook quickly, stirring often. Add onions and garlic and cook until tender and limp. Add water and simmer slowly. Remove stems and seeds from chilies and chop very fine. Grind chilies in mortar and pestle. After meat, onion, and garlic has simmered 1 hour add chilies. Add ground comino, oregano and salt to mixture. Simmer another 2 hours. Skim off fat. Never cook frijoles (beans) with chilies and meat. Serve as a separate dish.

*Sandie Smallwood*

# Chinese Pepper Steak

1 pkg. onion soup mix
1 1/2 cups boiling water
4 Tbsp. oil
1 lb. green peppers,
cut in eighths
1 lb. flank steak,
sliced thin
crosswise

1 clove garlic, crushed
1 Tbsp. soy sauce
1 Tbsp. sherry
2 Tbsp. cornstarch
3 Tbsp. cold water
Hot cooked rice

Combine onion soup mix and boiling water; let stand until ready to use. Heat 2 Tbsp. oil in a skillet and sauté green peppers one minute; remove. Add remaining oil and sauté garlic one minute; remove. Stir in meat and brown over high heat, turning while browning. Pour onion soup mixture, soy sauce, and sherry over meat. Stir in green peppers. Thicken with cornstarch mixed with cold water. Serve over hot rice. Serves 4.

*Charlotte Brown*

# Daddy's Favorite Round Steak

- 1¹/₂-2 lbs. round steak or venison steak, thinly sliced
- ¹/₄-¹/₂ cup Dijon mustard
- ²/₃ cup flour, seasoned with salt and pepper
- ¹/₄ cup oil
- 1 medium onion, chopped
- 1 clove garlic, chopped
- ¹/₂ cup bell pepper, chopped
- ¹/₂ cup celery, chopped
- 1 15 oz. can tomato sauce
- 1 Tbsp. worcestershire sauce
- Dash of Tabasco sauce
- ¹/₄ cup water

Cut round steak into 2"x4" pieces, discarding any fat or gristle. Cover each side of the meat with Dijon mustard and then dredge in the seasoned flour. Brown the meat in the oil and place in a large covered casserole, reserving the oil. In the reserved oil, sauté the onion, garlic, bell pepper, and celery. When vegetables are soft, but not brown, add the tomato sauce, worcestershire sauce, and Tabasco. Stir well and add the water. Pour the sauce over the meat and cover. Bake at 350 degrees for 1-1¹/₂ hours, depending on thickness of meat. The meat will be very tender and the sauce thickens during baking. This is delicious served with buttered noodles.

*Karen Bergnus Laurence*

# Farm Style Casserole

*(This Is So Good On A Cold Winter Day.)*

- ¹/₂ lb. hot sausage
- ¹/₂ lb. ground beef
- ²/₃ cup finely chopped onion
- 2 cups finely sliced celery
- 4 cups thinly sliced raw potatoes
- ¹/₂ cup fine, dry bread crumbs mixed with 2 tsp. parsley sprinkled with 2 tsp. vegetable oil

CHEESE SAUCE:
- 3 Tbsp. butter or margarine
- 3 Tbsp. flour
- ¹/₂ tsp. salt
- ¹/₂ tsp. pepper
- 2 cups milk
- 1 cup grated cheddar cheese

Melt butter over medium heat; stir in flour, salt and pepper. Gradually stir in milk and cook, stirring approximately 5 minutes. Add cheese. Preheat oven to 375 degrees. Sauté sausage and ground beef with onion and celery 20 minutes until brown. Drain excess fat. Layer meats with potatoes, salt, pepper, and cheese sauce in 2¹/₂ qt. casserole. Finish with cheese sauce. Mix crumbs, parsley and oil and sprinkle over top. Cover tightly and bake 1¹/₄ hours; uncover and bake 30 minutes.

*Doris Smith*

# Donna's Lasagne

1 medium onion, chopped
2 cloves garlic, minced
1 Tbsp. canola oil
1 lb. lean ground beef
1 lb. part-skim ricotta cheese or low fat cottage cheese
1/4 cup grated parmesan cheese
6 to 8 oz. part-skim mozzarella cheese, grated
2 cups sliced yellow and/or zucchini squash or 1 pkg. frozen spinach, chopped, thawed and drained

2 egg whites, beaten
1/4 tsp. black pepper, freshly ground
3 Tbsp. fresh parsley, chopped
1/2 lb. lasagne noodles
1 can Italian stewed tomatoes
1 15 oz. jar of garlic and herb prepared spaghetti sauce
Non stick vegetable cooking spray

Sauté the onion and garlic in the oil. Brown the lean ground meat. If the beef has fat, drain it off and pat the beef dry with paper towels. Combine the ricotta, parmesan, beef, squash or spinach, egg whites, pepper, parsley, onions, and garlic, mixing well. Cook the lasagna noodles according to directions. Spray or grease a 13"x9"x2" inch glass casserole dish. Arrange a layer of cooked noodles on the bottom; top with 1/3 of the Ricotta mixture; sprinkle with mozzarella cheese, and spread with tomato sauce. Repeat layers twice more, ending with sauce. Cover with aluminum foil, crimping edges tightly. Bake at 350 degrees for 40 minutes. Uncover and bake 10 to 15 minutes. Serves 12. 215 calories per serving.

*Donna Jackson*

# Filet Of Beef With Green Peppercorn Sauce

| | |
|---|---|
| 1 Tbsp. oil | 2 coarsely chopped carrots |
| 1 coarsely chopped medium yellow onion | |
| 1 4 lb. filet of beef, well trimmed | |

**SAUCE:**

| | |
|---|---|
| 7 Tbsp. butter | |
| 4 Tbsp. flour | |
| 1/4 cup green peppercorns, drained | |
| 1 1/2 cups beefstock | |
| 1/3 cup Madeira | |
| 3 Tbsp. brandy | |
| 1 cup heavy cream | |
| 1 tsp. lemon juice | |
| 1 tsp. salt | |
| 1/2 tsp. Tabasco | |

Preheat oven to 500 degrees. In a large, shallow roasting pan, on stove top, over high heat, heat oil; sauté carrots and onion, stirring constantly 2 minutes. Remove from heat. Place filet on top of vegetables. Roast 5 minutes. Reduce heat to 350 degrees and cook 40 minutes. Transfer to a carving board, cover loosely with foil, and let rest 20 minutes.

In a Dutch oven, heat 4 tablespoons butter and gradually add flour, stirring constantly until roux is light brown. Remove from heat, and gradually stir in $3/4$ cup stock. Over low heat, stir in remaining $3/4$ cup stock and Madeira: simmer 15 minutes. Keep warm. (Sauce may be prepared ahead of time up to this point.) Add pan drippings, brandy, and cream to sauce and bring to a boil. Cook, stirring 2 minutes. Reduce heat; add peppercorns, lemon juice, salt, Tabasco, and remaining 3 tablespoons butter; cook, stirring constantly 5 minutes. Carve filet in $3/4$ inch slices; arrange on a heated platter and spoon some green peppercorn sauce over slices. Serve remaining sauce in a heated sauceboat.

*Susan Muncey*

# Mrs. Day's Beef Brisket

| | |
|---|---|
| 8 lbs. or larger beef brisket (smaller briskets tend to be not as tender) | Salt and pepper |
| | Flour |
| | 1 can of beer |

Salt, pepper, and dust with flour. Put in large baking pan. Cover with can of beer. Cook, uncovered in 275 to 300 degree oven 1 hour per pound. At the end pour 1 can of mushroom soup over top. This makes delicious gravy makings.

*Doris Schmid*

# French Beef And Vegetable Casserole

6 slices bacon
1 lb. lean beef chuck, about 1/2" thick
1/2 cup flour
1 tsp. salt
1 cup dry red wine
2 Tbsp. parsley
1/2 garlic clove
1/2 tsp. thyme
1 10 1/2 oz. can condensed beef broth

6 medium potatoes, peeled and halved
12 small white onions, peeled
3 carrots, sliced lengthwise
1 4 oz. can mushroom stems and pieces, finely chopped

Cook bacon until crisp; drain on paper towels; reserve drippings. Cut beef into cubes. Shake a few cubes at a time in paper bag containing flour and salt. Brown cubes on all sides in bacon drippings; remove to 2-quart casserole. Pour wine into electric blender; add parsley, garlic, thyme, and beef broth; blend until solid ingredients are puréed. Pour over meat in casserole. Cover casserole; bake at 350 degrees for 1 hour. Stir potatoes, onions, and carrots into casserole. Replace cover. Bake 1 hour longer or until vegetables are done. Stir in mushrooms. Crumble bacon; scatter on top with additional chopped parsley. Makes 4 to 5 serving.

*Gretchen McWilliams*

*As mother used to say: Whatever you spend on convenience food at the grocery store, it's still cheaper than eating out.*

# Green Chile Lasagne

1 lb. lasagne noodles
1 Tbsp. butter or
  margarine
3 lbs. ground beef
40 oz. tomato sauce
1 Tbsp. sugar
1 tsp. garlic salt
Dash of pepper
2 cups cottage cheese
8 oz. cream cheese
1 cup sour cream
2 4 oz. cans green
  chilies, chopped
1 cup sliced green
  onions
Parmesan cheese

Cook noodles, drain well and add butter. Brown beef, drain and set aside. In large sauce pan combine tomato sauce, sugar, garlic salt, and pepper. Add meat and simmer until meat is tender (30 minutes). Skim off grease. Set aside. Mix remaining ingredients in a large mixing bowl until soft and creamy. Fill two 9"x13"x2" greased glass baking dishes by layering ingredients and topping with heavy layer of parmesan cheese. Cook in 350 degree oven for 45 minutes. (It is better prepared ahead.) Cover with foil and refrigerate if not ready to bake.

*Jan Fritz*

# Italian Beef And Peppers

1 lb. beef (flank or
  sirloin), sliced thin
2 Tbsp. olive oil
2 med. onions, sliced
1/2 cup water
1 or 2 large cloves of
  garlic, crushed
4 cups canned
  tomatoes
1 tsp. sugar
2 tsp. dried basil
1/8 tsp. pepper
1/4 tsp. salt
2 large green peppers,
  sliced thin
1/4 cup sherry

Sauté thin strips beef in oil until exuded juices cook dry and meat browns slightly. Add onions, garlic, and water. Cover tightly. Cook on low heat until meat is tender (about 5 minutes). Add rest of ingredients except green peppers. Cook 30 minutes. Add green peppers and cook covered 20 minutes longer. Serve over fresh buttered Italian (or French) bread or dunk bread in the sauce while eating. Serves 4-5.

*Angela Poen*

# Mexican Lasagna

1 lb. lean ground beef
1 16 oz. can refried beans
2 tsp. dried oregano
1 tsp. ground cumin
3/4 tsp. garlic powder
12 uncooked lasagna noodles
2 1/2 cups water
2 1/2 cups picante sauce or salsa
2 cups 16 oz. sour cream
3/4 cups finely sliced green onions
1 can sliced black olives drained
1 cup shredded monterey jack cheese

Combine beef, beans, oregano, cumin, and garlic powder. Place four of the uncooked lasagna noodles in the bottom of a 13"x9"x2" baking pan. Spread half the beef mixture over the noodles. Top with four more noodles and the remaining beef mixture. Cover with remaining noodles. Combine water and picante sauce. Pour over all. Cover tightly with foil; bake at 350 degrees for 1 1/2 hours or until noodles are tender. Combine sour cream, onions and olives. Spoon over casserole, top with cheese. Bake, uncovered, until cheese is melted, about 5 minutes. Serves 12.

*Dorothy Russell*

# Oven Brisket

6-10 lb. trimmed brisket
Mop Sauce (make a day ahead)
10 3/4 oz. can beef consommé
3/4 cup worcestershire sauce
1/3 cup cider vinegar
1 1/2 cup water
1/3 cup oil
1 1/2 tsp. MSG, optional
1 1/2 tsp. garlic powder
1 1/2 tsp. chili powder
1/2 tsp. tabasco
3 bay leaves
1/2 tsp. paprika

Bring all ingredients to boil — cover and let set overnight.

1/4 cup salt
1/3 cup chili powder
2 1/2 Tbsp. MSG
1 3/4 Tbsp. black pepper
1 1/2 Tbsp. garlic powder

Mix salt, chili powder, MSG, black pepper, garlic powder and roll trimmed beef in dry mix. Bake at 250 degrees. Mop before baking and again each hour and before serving. Bake 1 hour per pound, uncovered. Slice cold or hot — tastes great reheated.

*Linda Campbell*

# Popover Pizza

1/2 lb. pork sausage
1/2 lb. lean ground beef
15 oz. can tomato sauce
1 cup plus 2 Tbsp. all purpose flour
1 tsp. oregano
1/2 tsp. salt
3/4 lb. mozzarella cheese, sliced
2 eggs or egg whites
1 cup milk
1 Tbsp. corn oil
1/4 cup freshly grated parmesan cheese

Preheat oven to 425 degrees. Sauté meat until brown and crumbly. Drain excess fat. Add tomato sauce, 2 Tbsp. flour, oregano, and 1/4 tsp. salt. Pour into 13"x9" baking pan; cover with mozzarella slices. Beat eggs with milk, oil, remaining 1/4 tsp. salt, and 1 cup flour; pour over meat and cheese. Sprinkle with parmesan cheese. Bake until pizza is puffy and cheese melted about 25 to 30 minutes.

*Matthew Smith*

# South Texas Picadillo

1/2 lb. ground beef
1/2 lb. ground pork
1/2 small onion chopped
2 garlic cloves minced
2 Tbsp. fresh cilantro chopped
6 green olives pitted and chopped
2 tsp. capers chopped
1 medium tomato peeled and chopped

Combine beef and pork in large skillet. Salt and pepper to taste. Cook until meat is no longer pink, pressing and turning with a wooden spoon to keep crumbly. Drain excess fat from skillet then add remaining ingredients. Cook over medium heat 8 minutes stirring often.

Picadillo may be served with flavored rice or used as a filling for empanadas.

*Denice Miller Gruy*

# Santa Fe Beef Pasta Toss

2 lbs. beef tenderloin, cooked
1 cup julienned sundried tomatoes
1 cup diced tomatoes
3 bunches green onions, white part only, cut 1" pieces
1 cup fresh corn kernels
1 cup jicama
3/4 lb. cooked linguini noodles
DRESSING:
8 large cloves garlic
1 cup lime juice
3 medium jalapeños (for milder flavor do not use seeds)
1 Tbsp. plus 1 tsp. salt

1 Tbsp. sugar
1 bunch cilantro
22 oz. tomato juice or Bloody Mary mix
1/2 Tbsp. ground cumin
1/2 Tbsp. chili powder
Ground red pepper to taste
3 bunches green onions, white part only, cut in 1" pieces
3/4 cup olive oil
GARNISH:
8 oz. crumbled goat cheese
Cilantro
Red pepper slices

To prepare dressing, place all ingredients except oil in food processor and chop coarsely. While machine is running add oil. Toss dressing with remaining ingredients except garnish. Slice loin thinly (you may use left-over roast), combine with tomatoes, onions, corn, jicama, and noodles. Warm the mixture slowly in a skillet over medium-high heat, tossing to distribute the heat slowly and evenly. Place the heated mixture on a platter. Garnish with goat cheese, cilantro, and peppers, if desired. Serves 8 to 10.

*Diane Matthews*

# Weiner Schnitzel

*(Breaded Veal Cutlet)*

| | |
|---|---|
| **2 veal cutlets** | **1 beaten egg** |
| **Flour** | **Salt and pepper** |
| **³/₄ cup bread crumbs** | |

Flour veal and dip in beaten egg, remove carefully and coat with bread crumbs seasoned with salt and pepper. Let stand 5 minutes. Fry at medium heat for 3-4 minutes turning several times without piercing meat. Remove with tongs onto paper towels. Serve with brown gravy.

*Angela Poen*

# Sauerbraten for 20

| | |
|---|---|
| **1 rump roast, 4¹/₂ to 5 pounds** | **¹/₂ tsp. pepper** |
| **1¹/₂ cups red wine vinegar** | **¹/₂ tsp. ground cloves** |
| **1¹/₂ cups water** | **1 bay leaf** |
| **¹/₄ cup firmly packed light brown sugar** | **3 medium onions, chopped** |
| **2 tsp. salt** | **1¹/₂ cups chopped celery** |
| | **³/₄ cups gingersnap crumbs** |

In a large bowl or non-metal container, place roast. vinegar, water, brown sugar, salt, pepper, cloves, bay leaf, onions, and celery. Cover and refrigerate 2 or 3 days, turning meat occasionally in marinade. When ready to cook, remove meat from marinade. (save marinade), onto paper towels. Pat dry. Brown meat well on all sides in dutch oven over medium heat, adding some oil if needed. Add all the marinade. Heat to boiling, cover and simmer over low heat 2 hours or until fork tender. Remove to warm platter; keep warm. Strain marinade, reserving 4 cups. Skim off and discard any fat. Return the 4 cups of liquid to pot, sprinkle with gingersnap crumbs. Cook over medium heat, stirring until mixture thickens. For thinner gravy and more liquid. Salt to taste if desired.

*Alethia Alt*

# Spicy Meat Turnovers

2 pie crusts
4 Tbsp. raisins
4 Tbsp. olive oil
2 medium onions, finely chopped
2 large cloves garlic, minced
1 1/2 lbs. lean ground beef
Salt and pepper
2 Tbsp. parsley, minced
1/4 tsp. oregano
1/2 tsp. paprika
2 tsps. ground cumin
4 Tbsp. dry white wine
4 tsps. tomato sauce
1 hard boiled egg, minced

Cover raisins in warm water soak for 10 minutes. Heat oil in skillet. Sauté onions and garlic until soft. Add meat, cook and stir until just done. Drain off excess grease, salt and pepper to taste. Dry raisins, add to skillet with parsley, oregano, paprika, cumin, wine, tomato sauce, and hard boiled egg. Cover and cook slowly for 5 minutes. Either fill a double crust pie with mixture and bake until done, bake at 400 degrees for 30 minutes, or cut crust into individual serving size. Fill into double crusted turnovers and bake on cookie sheet until done, or cut crust into hors d'oeuvres size. Fill like mini turnovers. Bake on ungreased cookie sheet.

*Susan Muncey*

# Sweet And Sour Meatballs

1 lb. ground beef, or 1/2 lb. venison and 1/2 lb. beef
1 beaten egg, or 2 egg whites
2 Tbsp. oil or shortening
1 green pepper (cut in strips)
1 onion, sliced
1 1/2 cups pineapple juice, or 8 oz. can crushed pineapple
1/4 cup Heinz 57 sauce

Form meat into 16 meatballs. Brown in oil or shortening. Add green pepper and onions. Sauté until vegetables are tender. Add pineapple juice. Cover and simmer 20 minutes. Thicken with cornstarch. Serve over rice or noodles.

*C.C. Gibbons*

# Tijuana Torte

| | |
|---|---|
| 1 lb. lean ground beef | 4 oz. chopped green |
| 1 onion, chopped | chilies |
| 16 oz. can stewed | 1 and 1/4 oz. taco |
| tomatoes | seasoning mix |
| 8 oz. can tomato | 12 corn tortillas |
| sauce | 1 lb. cheddar cheese, |
| | grated |

Brown beef and onion. Drain. Add tomatoes, sauce, chilies, and taco mix. Simmer 15 minutes. Place 1/4 cup of meat mixture in the bottom of 13"x9"x2" pan. Put in 3 tortillas side by side the length of the pan and spoon some meat on each. Add a layer of cheese. Repeat until each tortilla has 4 layers of tortillas, meat, and cheese. Bake at 350 degrees 20-25 minutes. Cut each torte into wedges. Serves 6.

*Sharon Shiflet*

# Veal Taormina

| | |
|---|---|
| 2 eggs, beaten | 24 oz. can tomato |
| 1 1/2 cups seasoned | sauce |
| breadcrumbs | 2 tsp. sugar |
| 1 large eggplant, pared | 1 tsp. oregano |
| and sliced in | 1/2 tsp. basil |
| 1/4" slices | 1/2 tsp. salt |
| 3/4 cup olive oil | 1/2 cup parmesan |
| 1 1/2 lb. veal, ground | cheese |
| once | 8 oz. sliced mozzarella |
| | cheese |

Preheat oven to 350 degrees. Dip eggplant slices in eggs and then into bread crumbs. Fry in oil and drain on paper towels. Shape veal into a large patty and brown 5 minutes on each side. Break patty into chunks and stir in tomato sauce, sugar, oregano, basil and salt. Simmer 10 minutes. Place 1/3 of egg-plant in a greased 13"x9"x2" baking dish, cover with 1/3 meat sauce, add 1/3 of parmesan cheese and 1/3 of the mozzarella cheese. Repeat until all ingredi-ents are used. Bake 40 minutes or until cheese is bubbly. Serves 8-10.

*Susan Muncey*

# Baked Chicken With Red Sauce

**1 chicken (about 3-4 lbs.)**

**1 cup white wine**
**¹/₂ cup olive oil**

Cut chicken in half splitting the breast. Remove the backbone. Lay the 2 halves flat, skin side up, in a shallow baking pan. Rub them all over with olive oil; salt and pepper to taste. Bake 50-55 minutes at 425 degrees, basting occasionally with white wine.

**RED SAUCE:**
**¹/₂ tsp. rosemary, ground fine**
**¹/₄ tsp. dried oregano,**
**1 tsp. dried basil.**
**Put in sauce pan with:**
**1 16 oz. can tomatoes**

**¹/₂ lemon rind, grated**
**Piece of cinnamon stick**
**Pinch of sugar**
**Fresh ground pepper to taste**

Put rosemary, oregano, basil, tomatoes, lemon rind, sugar, cinnamon, and pepper in sauce pan and bring to a boil, chopping tomatoes with a wooden spoon. Cook until volume is reduced by half. Turn off fire. Add 2 or 3 Tbsp. butter, salt to taste. Add this sauce around the chicken the last 10 minutes of baking. (This sauce is so good I double it.) Serve with a side dish of pasta. Serves 4.

*Christina Straka*

*The Italians say: Fish of an hour, bread of a day, and a friend of thirty years.*

# Chicken And Rice

3 cups cooked
chicken, boned and
cut in pieces
1 box Uncle Ben's Wild
and White Rice
1 can cream of celery
soup
1 4 oz. jar sliced
pimientos
1 medium onion
chopped
2 cups French cut
string beans,
drained
1 cup mayonnaise
1 pkg. almonds,
slivered
1 can water chestnuts,
drained and diced
Salt and pepper to
taste

Cook rice according to package (for better flavor use chicken broth instead of water). Mix all the ingredients together, pour into 2½ to 3 qt. casserole. Bake 30 minutes at 350 degrees. (To freeze do not bake before freezing.) Serves 14.

*Charleen Miller*
*Mary Lois Clark*

# Chicken Cordon Bleu

*(Italian Style)*

2 skinned and boned
chicken breasts cut
in half
2 oz. (4 slices) lean
boiled ham
4 oz. (4 slices)
mozzarella cheese
1 tsp. oregano
Onion or garlic powder
Salt and fresh ground
pepper
1 cup chicken broth
(fat skimmed off)
4 Tbsp. tomato paste
2 Tbsp. white wine,
optional
3 Tbsp. grated, sharp
romano cheese

Pound breasts into cutlets. Place ham and cheese slices on each breast. Sprinkle lightly with seasonings. Roll up (ham and cheese on inside) and secure with toothpick. Place seam side down in greased baking dish. Combine broth, tomato paste, and wine, stirring until smooth. Pour over chicken. Bake at 425 degrees in pre-heated oven 15-20 minutes. Sprinkle on romano cheese. Serves 4.

*Danye Dolan Alt*

# Chicken Breasts In Wine Sauce

4 chicken breast
   halves, skinned and
   boned
5¹/₂ cups chicken
   broth, defatted
4 medium carrots,
   pared and julienned
2 celery stalks,
   chopped
2 medium red onions,
   sliced
Bouquet garni*
8 whole peppercorns

2 or 3 cloves of garlic
¹/₂ cup white wine
3 sprigs tarragon or
   ¹/₂ tsp. dried
2 shallots, chopped
¹/₂ cup whipping
   cream or sour
   cream
2 Tbsp. butter
   (optional)

*4 parsley sprigs,
   1 bay leaf, 1 thyme
   tied together

Combine broth, carrots, celery, onions, and bouquet garni in large saucepan. Bring to a boil, add peppercorns, and garlic. Cook over medium high heat for 20 minutes. Add chicken, cook 8 to 10 minutes, until cooked through. Do not overcook. Set chicken aside on a platter, cover to keep warm. Strain two cups broth from pan, set aside. Leave vegetables and remaining broth in pan, cover to keep warm. Make a wine sauce in a smaller saucepan by combining 2 cups of the strained broth with wine, tarragon, and chopped shallots. Cook until reduced by half (this can be done earlier). Strain. Return to pan. Bring to boil, add whipping cream and cook until it is reduced, whisking often. Sauce is done when it coats spoon. Add two Tbsp. butter. Pour sauce over chicken. Serve vegetables in a separate bowl.

*Angela Poen*

# Chicken Breast Stuffed With Sun Dried Tomatoes And Cheese

| | |
|---|---|
| 2 Tbsp. goat cheese | 3/4 tsp. ground pepper |
| 2 tsp. sun-dried tomatoes, chopped | 1/4 tsp. minced garlic |
| 2 chicken breasts, skinned and boned | 2 tsp. chopped parsley |
| | 1/4 cup bread crumbs |
| | 1/4 tsp. salt |
| | 1 egg white, beaten |

In small bowl, mash cheese, tomatoes, parsley, garlic, and 1/4 tsp. of the pepper. Cut a 2" long pocket in the side of each breast and fill with cheese mixture. Mix bread crumbs with 1/4 tsp. salt and 1/4 tsp. pepper. Brush chicken with the beaten egg white and dredge in bread crumbs. Refrigerate breasts for 15 minutes. In skillet, melt butter over medium high heat. Add chicken. Turn until evenly coated with butter. Lower heat, cover and simmer 3 minutes on one side. Turn breasts over, cover and cook until chicken is just white throughout, but still moist (about 4 more minutes). Good served on warm plates with steamed nutmeg-seasoned spinach.

*Variation: Instead of slitting breasts, pound them thin between sheets of waxed paper. Spread cheese mixture on one side and fold over.*

*Martha Kipcak*

# Chicken Cacciatore

*(Microwave)*

1 medium onion,
    chopped
1 green bell pepper,
    thinly sliced
1 Tbsp. butter
1 28 oz. can whole
    tomatoes
$1/4$ cup all purpose
    flour
1 bay leaf
1 Tbsp. dried parsley

1 tsp. salt
1 clove garlic, minced
$1/2$ tsp. oregano
1 tsp. paprika
$1/4$ tsp. pepper
$1/4$ tsp. basil
$1/2$ cup dry red wine,
    or water
1 chicken $2^1/2$ to 3
    pounds, cut up*

In a 3 quart micro-casserole, combine onion, green pepper, and butter. Cook, covered, on high 4 to 5 minutes, until onion is transparent. Add tomatoes and flour, stir until smooth. Stir in all remaining ingredients except chicken. Cook, covered, on high 5 minutes. Add chicken pieces immersing in sauce. Cover, cook on high, 25 minutes, or until chicken is tender, stirring once during cooking. Let stand 5 minutes, covered. Remove bay leaf. Serves 4-6. Good with pasta or rice.

*\* Substitute 3 cups of skinless and boneless chicken cut in bite size pieces. Cut cooking time to 15 minutes.*

*Patti Richard*

## Chicken Divan

| | |
|---|---|
| 2 pkgs. frozen broccoli or 1 bunch fresh broccoli | cream of chicken soup |
| 2 cups sliced chicken (cooked) | 1 cup mayonnaise |
| 2 cans condensed | 1 tsp. lemon juice |
| | $1/_2$-1 tsp. curry powder |
| | $1/_2$ cup grated sharp cheese |
| | $1/_2$ Tbsp. melted butter |
| | $1/_2$ cup bread crumbs |

The melted butter and bread crumbs may be omitted. Cook broccoli in boiling, salted water until tender, drain. Arrange stalks of broccoli in greased pyrex baking dish with flowerets facing outward. Place chicken on top of broccoli. Combine soup, mayonnaise, lemon juice, and curry powder. Pour over chicken, sprinkle with cheese and bread crumbs. Bake 350 degree oven for 25-30 minutes.

*Bobbye Swatzky*

*Ruby Edwards adds a few strips of pimiento on top of hers.*

## Chicken Floretta

| | |
|---|---|
| 1 large chicken cooked, deboned, cut in pieces | 1 pt. $1/_2$ & $1/_2$ cream |
| 1 4 oz. can sliced ripe olives | $1 1/_2$ cups grated sharp cheese (save $1/_2$ cup for topping) |
| 1 4 oz. can sliced mushrooms | 1 stick butter or margarine |
| 1 4 oz. pkg. slivered almonds | $1/_2$ cup flour |
| | $1/_2$ cup sherry |
| | $1/_2$ cup cracker crumbs |

Cook cream, 1 cup of the cheese, butter, and flour in double-boiler to make a thick sauce, then add sherry. Mix chicken, olives, mushrooms, and almonds into sauce. Pour into casserole, cover with cracker crumbs and $1/_2$ cup of cheese, dot with butter. Bake at 350 degrees until bubbly (20 or 30 min.) Serve over cooked rice.

*Ruth Holman*

# Chicken Olympic

4 chicken breasts, split, or 1 whole small chicken
3 quarts water
1 small onion, chopped
2 celery stalks, chopped
1 bay leaf
Salt and pepper to taste
8 oz. of coleslaw dressing
1 cup mayonnaise
2 tsp. curry powder
1 11 oz. can mandarin oranges, drained
1 15¹/₄ oz. can pineapple chunks
1 cup white raisins
2 oz. slivered almonds

Cook chicken in water with celery, onion, and bay leaf. Skin, debone and cut into bite size pieces. Put in a 2 quart baking dish. Mix together coleslaw dressing, mayonnaise, curry, oranges, pineapple, and raisins. Pour over chicken. Top with almonds. Bake at 350 degrees in pre-heated oven 30 minutes. This can be prepared a day ahead, and baked before serving. Serves 8.

*Trudy Harris*

# Chicken Parmesan

4 chicken breast halves, skinned and boned
Salt, pepper, garlic powder, and flour
4 slices of provolone or mozzarella slices
2 Tbsp. olive oil
1 Tbsp. butter
¹/₂ cup grated parmesan
2 cups prepared spaghetti sauce or homemade sauce

Pound to flatten chicken breasts between two sheets of plastic or wax paper. Season and flour lightly. Brown chicken lightly on both sides in a skillet with oil and butter. Before removing chicken cover each piece with sliced cheese. Place breasts in shallow casserole and cover with tomato sauce. Sprinkle parmesan over sauce. Bake in 350 degrees oven 15 to 20 minutes or in the microwave for 4 minutes on high, or until cheese melts. Serves 4.

*Taylor Miller*
*Tom Alt*

# Chicken Salad Tujacue

4 whole chicken
breasts
1 14 oz. can chicken
broth or 1 pint
chicken stock
1 tsp. salt
1/4 tsp. pepper
1 cup Italian salad
dressing
2 cups celery, finely
chopped

Simmer chicken breasts in broth or stock with salt and pepper until real tender, about 20-25 minutes. Remove skin and bones and cut in bite size pieces. Marinate chicken in salad dressing overnight. Next day prepare remaining ingredients. Mix and chill. Serves 6-8.

*Charleen Miller*

# Cranberry Chicken

3 pounds chicken
thighs
1 cup flour
Salt and pepper to
taste
4-6 Tbsp. melted
butter or margarine
1 1/2 cups fresh
cranberries
3/4 cup sugar
1/4 cup chopped onion
1 tsp. grated orange
peel
3/4 cup orange juice
1/4 tsp. cinnamon
1/4 tsp. ground ginger
4 Tbsp. butter

1 shallot, finely
chopped
2 hard boiled eggs,
finely chopped
1/4 cup toasted almond
slivers
1/2 cup (scant)
mayonnaise
1/4 tsp. mustard
Salt and pepper to
taste

Coat chicken with seasoned flour and brown in a skillet with melted butter over medium heat. Remove and place thighs in 13"x9" baking dish. Combine remaining ingredients in a large saucepan, bring to boil 2 to 3 minutes. Pour sauce over chicken. Cover and bake 45 minutes at 300 degrees. Delicious served over a cooked long grain and wild rice mix. Great company dish because it holds well in oven until serving time.

*Karen B. Laurence*

# Forgotten Chicken

1 cup uncooked rice
2 cans cream of
   chicken soup
1¹/₂ cups water
1 large fryer, cut in
   pieces

Salt and pepper to
   taste
¹/₂ pkg. dry onion
   soup mix

Pre-heat oven to 350 degrees. Place rice in bottom of a shallow, greased casserole. Combine soup and water. Pour some of the soup mixture over the rice, and let stand a few minutes. Place chicken pieces on top of rice. Salt and pepper. Pour remaining soup over it. Top with onion mixture. Cover, put in hot oven and forget about it for 1¹/₂ to 2 hours. Serves 6.

*Ruby Edwards*

# Fruited Chicken

4 chicken breasts
¹/₂ cup apricot halves
1 16 oz. can pineapple
   chunks, drained
2 green onions,
   chopped

5 Tbsp. sweet and sour
   sauce
2 Tbsp. worcestershire
   sauce
2 Tbsp. water

Place chicken in baking dish. Spread fruit and onions on top. Mix remaining ingredients and pour over. Bake covered at 325 degrees for 1 hour.

*Betsy Slyker*

## Garlic Chicken

| | |
|---|---|
| 6-8 boneless chicken breast portions | 1/2 cup cooking wine |
| 1 cup bread crumbs or crushed corn flakes | 1/4 stick butter or margarine |
| 3 eggs | 1 or 2 cloves minced garlic |
| Sliced mozzarella cheese | 1 package frozen broccoli spears |
| | 2 cans whole potatoes (or fresh cooked potato chunks) |
| | 1/4 cup oil |

Beat eggs in a pie plate. Pour bread crumbs or crushed corn flakes into a separate plate or into a sealable plastic bag. Dip chicken into egg, then into bread crumbs until both sides are evenly coated. Brown chicken pieces in hot oil; arrange pieces into 13"x9"x2" baking dish. Place a broccoli spear on top of each chicken piece. Drain potatoes and arrange around chicken. Melt butter with cooking wine and garlic. Pour mixture over chicken and vegetables; top with slices of mozzarella cheese. Bake at 350 degrees for 30 minutes or until chicken is done.

*Linda Kager*

## Hedery's Chicken

| | |
|---|---|
| 1 whole chicken, quartered, or 4 breasts | 3 or 4 carrots, quartered, 3" or 4" long slices |
| Olive oil, salt and dried oregano | 4 cloves garlic, peeled |
| 2 potatoes, peeled and cut in large chunks | 2 large lemons, squeezed |
| | 3 fresh tomatoes, quartered |

Rinse and dry chicken. Place in baking pan, drizzle oil over and sprinkle with salt and oregano. Add potatoes and carrots, bake uncovered 475-500 degrees (yes, that hot!) for 30 minutes. Meanwhile, measure lemon juice and add equal amount of olive oil. Mash or press garlic, stir into juice and oil. When chicken is done add tomatoes to pan and pour lemon-oil over it all. Return to oven for 5-6 minutes.

*Barbara Alt Smith*

# Georgia Brunswick Stew

2 (2 to 3 lb.) frying
  chickens
Hot water (to cover)
1 8$^1/_2$ oz. can whole
  kernel corn
1 10 oz. pkg. frozen
  lima beans
1 10 oz. pkg. frozen okra
1$^1/_4$ tsp. Tabasco sauce
1 Tbsp. salt
$^1/_4$ lb. ham

2 medium onions,
  chopped
1 No. 2 can tomatoes
$^1/_2$ tsp. salt
$^1/_4$ tsp. thyme
$^1/_8$ tsp. pepper
1 small green pepper,
  chopped
3 Tbsp. butter or
  margarine
$^1/_4$ cup flour

Place chicken breasts down in heavy saucepan, with a tight fitting cover. Add hot water and salt. Bring to boil; reduce heat. Cover pan and simmer about 45 minutes. When chickens are tender, cool, then remove meat from bones. Return chicken meat to broth. Add ham, onions, tomatoes, corn, lima beans, okra, and all other ingredients, except green pepper, butter, and flour. Simmer for 2 or 3 hours until it thickens. Heat butter in saucepan: blend in flour until lightly browned. Stir this mixture into stew until thickened. Add green pepper and cook for 15 minutes.

*Doris Smith*

# Hot Chicken Salad

| | |
|---|---|
| 2 cups cooked chicken, chopped | 1 cup mayonnaise |
| 2 cups chopped celery | 2 Tbsp. lemon juice |
| ¹/₂ cup slivered almonds | ¹/₂ cup grated American cheese |
| ¹/₂ tsp. salt | 1 cup crushed potato chips |
| 2 Tbsp. grated onion | |

Mix all ingredients together, except one half of the cheese and potato chips. Put in baking dish and sprinkle remaining cheese and chips on top. Bake at 450 degrees for 15 minutes. Serves 4-6.

*Betty Ethel*

# Lemon Chicken Breast From "Mike And Charlie's"

| | |
|---|---|
| 6 (6 to 8 oz.) boneless chicken breasts | 1 cup olive oil |
| 6 cloves garlic (crushed) | 2¹/₄ tsp. rosemary |
| 4 or 5 lemons (freshly squeezed) | 1 Tbsp. coarse black pepper |
| | 1 Tbsp. salt |

Combine all ingredients except chicken breasts and mix well. Add chicken and marinate at least 12 hours, but not more than 24 hours. Drain (throw away marinade) and grill. This is especially delicious cooked over mesquite chips. Leave the skin on the chicken while cooking to keep it moist. If you want the skin removed, do so just before serving.
Delicious!

*Martha Kipcak*

# Mexican Pizza

2 1/2 cups cooked,
  skinned, boned and
  shredded chicken
1/2 cup chopped green
  onions
5 oz. fresh sliced
  mushrooms
1 cup oil
3 oz. tomato sauce
3 oz. picante sauce
1 tsp. ground cumin
  (cominos)
1/2 tsp. salt or to taste

1 15 oz. can refried
  beans
1/3 cup water
2 cups grated
  monterey jack
  cheese
8 oz. sour cream
12 or so slices
  jalapeño, optional
4 oz. guacamole
4 10 inch flour
  tortillas

In large skillet, sauté onion and mushrooms in 1/4 cup oil. Stir until onions soften. Add chicken, tomato sauce, picante, cumin, and salt. Simmer over low heat about 10 minutes, stirring often, until liquid is almost gone. Remove from heat, cover and set aside. (This can be made ahead, refrigerated, and warmed before using.) Fry tortillas in rest of oil in a 12 inch skillet until golden brown. Dry on paper towels. Heat refried beans, stirring in water. Spread tops of tortillas with beans. Cover each with 3/4 cup chicken mix. Sprinkle cheese over each. Place under broiler until cheese melts. Remove. Dot with sour cream and sliced jalapeños. In center of each put 1 Tbsp. guacamole. Serve immediately or tortillas will soften. A little trouble, but you will get rave reviews!

*AUSLANDER RESTAURANT, Fredericksburg*

*The Greeks say: How can I remember you if you
do not eat at my table.*

# Oriental Chicken Salad

| | |
|---|---|
| **4 chicken breasts** | **SALAD:** |
| **1 pkg. Maifun noodles** | **1 medium size head of** |
| **Peanut oil for deep** | **lettuce** |
| **frying** | **4 green onions** |
| **DRESSING:** | **¹/₄ cup sesame seeds** |
| **4 Tbsp. sugar** | **¹/₂ cup toasted almond** |
| **4 Tbsp. wine vinegar** | **slices** |
| **2 tsp. salt** | |
| **¹/₈ tsp. black pepper.** | |
| **¹/₂ cup peanut oil** | |

Boil the four chickens breasts in water until tender. Drain, cool, and shred the chicken. Set aside. Deep fry the Maifun noodles in peanut oil. They will puff up and get crisp and brown in just a few seconds. Remove with a slotted spoon and drain on paper towels. Set aside. In a small saucepan, on medium heat, bring the following ingredients to a slow boil: sugar, wine vinegar, salt, and black pepper. Remove from heat and allow to cool a few minutes, then add ¹/₂ cup peanut oil and mix together. Using a very large mixing bowl, shred the lettuce into it. Slice the green onion into diagonal pieces and add. Add the sesame seeds, almonds and toss together. Add shredded chicken and toss. Add fried Maifun noodles and toss. Pour dressing over all and toss. Serve immediately. Will serve six.

*Jean Wieser*

# Oriental Chicken With Pineapple

4 chicken breast halves skinned and boned
2 Tbsp. margarine
1 8 oz. can tomato sauce (no salt)
1/2 cup sliced celery
1 medium onion, sliced
1 medium bell pepper, chopped
1/4 Tbsp. ground ginger
1 Tbsp. cornstarch
1/4 cup soy sauce
2 Tbsp. sherry
1 8 oz. can pineapple tidbits, reserving 1/4 cup juice
3 cups hot cooked rice

Cut chicken in bite size pieces. Allow wok or large skillet to heat at medium high for 2 minutes. Melt margarine in wok, add chicken, stir-fry 4 to 5 minutes until golden brown. Stir in vegetables, tomato sauce, cover, reduce heat, simmer 4-5 minutes. Mix reserved juice, cornstarch, and spices, cook until mixture is slightly thickened. Combine hot rice with drained pineapple. Serve chicken mix over rice. Serves 6.

*Elena Miller*

# Russian Chicken

8 chicken breast halves or thighs
1 8 oz. bottle Russian or Catalina salad dressing
2 envelopes dry onion soup mix
1 8 oz. Fredericksburg peach preserves (others will do, but of course, not as good)

Preheat oven to 300 degrees. Place chicken in a 13"x9" baking dish. Mix all remaining ingredients and spread over chicken. Bake for 1 1/2 hours or until chicken is done. Serve with rice. Serves 6 to 8.

*For the calorie and fat conscious, fat-free dressing and reduced sugar preserves may be substituted with the same delicious results.!*

*Karen Benignus Laurence*

# Stir-Fry Chicken With Walnuts

| | |
|---|---|
| 1 to 1¹/₂ lbs. chicken breasts (cut into 1″ pieces) | ¹/₄ tsp. salt |
| 3 Tbsp. soy sauce | 2 Tbsp. oil |
| 2 tsp. cornstarch | 2 green peppers (cut into ³/₄″ pieces) |
| 2 tsp. dry sherry | 4 green onions (cut into 1″ lengths) |
| 1 tsp. grated ginger | ²/₃ cup walnuts |
| ¹/₂ tsp. sugar | |

In small bowl, mix soy sauce into cornstarch. Stir in sherry, ginger, sugar, salt, and red pepper (optional). Preheat wok or large skillet and add oil. Stir fry peppers and onions for 2 minutes or until tender. Remove. Add walnuts to skillet, stir-fry 1 or 2 minutes. Remove. Add half of chicken, cook 2 minutes, remove and cook other half 2 minutes. Return chicken to wok, add soy mixture, and stir until thickened. Add veggies, cover, and cook 1 or 2 minutes more. Serve with rice.

Will probably need to add more oil as you cook the chicken.

*Jeannine Miller*

*A great way to diet is to grab your mate instead of your plate.*

# Charcoaled Bourbon — Marinated Lamb

| | |
|---|---|
| 1 medium leg of lamb, about 8 lbs. cut into 1/2" steaks | 3 large cloves garlic, chopped |
| 1 1/2 cups bourbon | 3 large onions, thinly sliced |
| 3/4 cup soy sauce | Garnish: Chutney, mustard, slivered green onions |
| 3/4 cup olive oil | |

Put the lamb steaks in non-metal container large enough to hold them comfortably. Combine the remaining ingredients and pour over lamb. Cover and refrigerate for at least 24 hours. Now and then give the steaks a turn.

An hour before you want to start cooking, take steaks out to reach room temperature. Arrange chops over a charcoal grill that has a large even bed of white coals. Cook 7 minutes on each side.

*Martha Kipcak*

# Peppered Raspberry Lamb Chops

| | |
|---|---|
| 4 lean lamb chops (1 inch thick, 4 oz. each) | 2 tsp. worcestershire sauce |
| 1/2 tsp. cracked pepper | 1 1/2 tsp. raspberry vinegar |
| 3 Tbsp. low sugar raspberry spread | 1/2 pint fresh raspberries |

Trim fat from chops. Press pepper into both sides of meat. Broil to desired doneness. Keep warm. combine remaining ingredients, except fresh raspberries, in a sauce pan. Cook over medium heat, stirring constantly, until spread melts. Spoon over warm chops. Garnish with fresh raspberries. Serves 4.

*Cay Meadows*

# Smothered Lamb Chops

*(If You Like Garlic, You Will Love This)*

4 large thick lamb
  chops
Salt and pepper
2 Tbsp. flour for
  coating
¹/₄ cup vegetable oil
3 or 4 cloves garlic
  minced
¹/₄ cup chopped
  parsley
1 cup canned
  tomatoes
¹/₃ cup tomato sauce
3 Tbsp. wine vinegar
¹/₄ cup dry white wine

Season chops with salt and pepper. Pound flour into chops. Heat oil in medium skillet and brown meat on both sides. Combine garlic and parsley in a small dish and spread on top of chops. In a bowl combine tomatoes, tomato sauce, vinegar and wine. Place 2 chops in skillet, top with half the tomato mixture. Stack other two chops on top and cover with remaining tomato mixture. Cover tightly and simmer for 1 hour. Serves 4.

*Alethia Alt*

# Venison Chili

2 lbs. coarsely ground
  venison
¹/₂ lb. pork, browned
  in ¹/₂ cup drippings
Salt and pepper to
  taste
1 medium onion,
  chopped
1¹/₂ Tbsp. chili powder
3 Tbsp. flour
1 cup tomato paste
  and enough water
  to cover
Garlic to taste

Simmer all together in a heavy pot, 1 hour, or until meat is tender.

*Bessie Evers*

'Tis an ill cook that cannot lick his own fingers.
    —*Shakespeare*

# Cavatini

1 lb. hot pork sausage
or ¹/₂ lb. mild and
¹/₂ hot
1 12 oz. pkg. Rotini
pasta
1 large green bell
pepper cut into
strips
1 2 oz. jar sliced
mushrooms

¹/₄ cup sliced onions
¹/₂ cup sliced, pitted
black olives
2 cups shredded
mozzarella cheese
2¹/₂ cups spaghetti
sauce, homemade
preferably
Parmesan cheese,
grated

Cook sausage, crumbling it up as it browns. Drain off excess grease and add green peppers and onions, cooking until translucent. Add mushrooms, olives and spaghetti sauce. Simmer until heated through, about 10 minutes. Meanwhile cook pasta until al dente, about 9 minutes. Drain. Pour pasta into greased 3 quart 13"x9"x2" casserole, shake parmesan liberally over hot pasta, then add sauce and mix well. This casserole tastes best if left to rest and absorb flavors, so it is excellent for families as it can be made in the morning and cooked later. Put shredded mozzarella cheese on top before baking. Bake 350 degrees 25-30 minutes, if it has been refrigerated add 15 minutes or till hot and bubbly. This keeps well and reheats in the microwave. Teenagers love it.

*Jeannine Miller*

*No man is lonely while eating spaghetti.*
*— Robert Morley*

# Cornmeal Scrapple

*(This Is An Old German Recipe
And A Family Favorite.)*

| | |
|---|---|
| 1 cup white or yellow cornmeal | 8 oz. pork sausage |
| 1 cup milk | $1/2$ cup flour |
| 1 tsp. sugar | 2 Tbsp. butter or margarine |
| 1 tsp. salt | Maple syrup, optional |
| $2^3/4$ cups boiling water | |

Cook, crumble, and drain sausage, set aside.

In saucepan, combine cornmeal, milk, sugar & salt; gradually stir in water. Cook and stir until thickened and bubbly. Reduce heat, cook, covered 10 min. longer or until very thick, stirring occasionally. Remove from heat and stir in sausage. Pour into greased $7^1/2$"x$3^1/2$"x$2$" loaf pan (the pan will be very full). Cover with plastic wrap and refrigerate. To serve, unmold and cut into $1/3$" slices. Dip both sides in flour. Melt butter in skillet over medium heat; brown scrapple on both sides. Serve with maple syrup if desired. Yields 6 servings.

*Dorothy Russell*

# Ham Balls

| | SAUCE: |
|---|---|
| 1 lb. ground ham | 1 cup brown sugar |
| 1 lb. lean ground pork | 1 tsp. dry mustard |
| 2 cups bread crumbs | $1/2$ cup vinegar |
| 2 well beaten eggs | $1/2$ cup water |
| 1 cup milk | |

Combine ham, pork, crumbs, egg, milk and shape into small balls. Mix sauce ingredients, heat over low fire stirring until sugar dissolves. Pour over ham balls. Baste and bake 1 hour at 350 degrees.

*Anita Page*

# Mrs. Wagener's Ham

**Butt end or rolled ham**
**Peach or pineapple**
   **juice**
**Mustard**

**Brown sugar**
**Cornmeal**
**Black pepper**

Simmer ham in about 1-2 inches of water in a covered container on the top of the stove 3-4 hours, depending on the size. Remove from fire, pour off water, make slits in the ham and pour sliced peach or pineapple juice over it. If possible, refrigerate overnight. Cover with mustard, then brown sugar, and sprinkle with cornmeal and pepper. Bake uncovered in slow oven 300-325 degrees for about 1 1/2 hours.

*Martha Craig*

# Souffléd Cheese Toast With Ham

**6 slices white bread,**
   **crusts removed**
**2 1/2 Tbsp. butter,**
   **softened**
**6 slices ham**
**18 asparagus spears,**
   **cooked**
**4 eggs, separated**
**1 tsp. dry mustard**

**1/4 tsp. worcestershire**
   **sauce**
**1/8 tsp. cayenne**
   **pepper**
**1 cup grated sharp**
   **cheddar cheese**
**1/4 tsp. salt**
**Pimiento strips, thinly**
   **sliced**

Preheat oven to 375 degrees. Toast bread and lightly butter one side. Place on greased baking sheet, topping each slice with 1 slice ham and 3 asparagus spears. In a bowl, beat egg yolks with dry mustard, worcestershire sauce and cayenne. Stir in cheese. In another bowl, beat egg whites with salt until stiff. Fold small amount of egg whites into cheese mixture. Fold in remaining whites. Spoon soufflé mixture over asparagus. Bake 10 minutes or until puffed and lightly browned. Garnish with pimiento strips. Serves 6.

*Susan Muncey*

# Porcupine Pork Roast

*(Start a day ahead)*

**1 7 lb. pork loin roast,**
**ribs cracked,**
**untrimmed**
**¹/₄ cup olive oil**
**1¹/₂ tsp. salt**
**1 tsp. pepper**
**1¹/₂ tsp. oregano**
**¹/₂ tsp. thyme**
**¹/₃ cup flour**
**2 onions, sliced**
**2 Tbsp. cornstarch**
**³/₄ cup water**

**BASTING SAUCE:**
**2¹/₄ cups water**
**3 beef bouillon cubes**
**2 chicken bouillon**
**cubes**
**1¹/₄ cups white wine**
**2 cloves garlic,**
**pressed**
**³/₄ cup sour cream,**
**room temperature**

With a knife, score fat in a diamond pattern. Rub roast with oil. Sprinkle with salt, pepper, oregano and thyme. Coat with flour. Arrange onions on scored surface and secure with toothpicks. Place in shallow roasting pan, cover tightly and refrigerate overnight. On day of serving, remove from refrigerator at least 1 hour prior to cooking. Preheat oven to 375 degrees and cook 30 minutes. In a saucepan, bring water to a boil and dissolve bouillon cubes. Reduce to low heat; add wine and garlic; simmer 5 minutes. Remove from heat and stir in sour cream. Reduce oven temperature to 325 degrees and pour sauce over roast. Cook 4 hours, basting every 30 minutes. Transfer to a heated serving platter, cover loosely with foil and let rest 15 minutes. In a cup, stir cornstarch in water. Place roasting pan on stove top; stir in cornstarch; simmer 10 minutes, scraping brown bits on bottom of pan. Serve in a heated sauceboat. Serves 6.

*Susan Muncey*

# Tequila Marinated Pork Tenderloins

**2 pork tenderloins, 1 pound each**
**4 cloves garlic, thickly sliced**
**3 Tbsp. fresh rosemary, chopped**

**MARINADE:**
**1 cup tequila**
**2 tsp. salt**
**1¹/₂ cups vegetable oil**
**1 Tbsp. black pepper**
**¹/₄ cup fresh lime juice**

Make several 1 inch deep slits in the tenderloins. Stuff the slits with garlic and rosemary. Combine the marinade ingredients and marinade the tenders for 8-10 hours or overnight, turning occasionally. Prepare charcoal grill, (adding some mesquite chips that have been soaked in water).

When coals are white-hot, put the tenderloins on the grill and cook 15-20 minutes, turning to grill evenly. Serves 4-6.

*Karen Benignus Laurence*

*Friendship is the wine of life.*

# Crab Cakes With Lime Butter

3 cups bread crumbs
1 lb. crabmeat
Juice of 1 lemon and 1 lime
1 small red and 1 small white onion, chopped
1 clove garlic, chopped
1 tsp. butter
1 green, 1 red pepper, chopped

1/2 cup mayonnaise
1/2 cup mustard
1 Tbsp. dry mustard
2 Tbsp. tabasco sauce
1 Tbsp. worcestershire sauce

LIME BUTTER:
4 Tbsp. butter
2 oz. butter
1/2 lime
1/8 tsp. minced chives

Remove all small pieces of shell from the crab meat. Combine the crab meat and the juice of the lemon and lime and let sit for 10 minutes. Meanwhile sauté the onion, garlic, and peppers until almost cooked completely, in butter. Combine the crab and sautéed vegetables together and mix. Add the mayonnaise, mustard, and dry mustard and mix. Mix in about 2 cups of bread crumbs in mixture. You need a consistency that is cohesive and dry enough not to stick to your hands. Form 3 to 3½ oz. cakes and roll in bread crumbs. Cook the cakes in butter until good and crispy on both sides, about 3 to 4 minutes a side. Serve hot with lime garnish. Serves 8 to 10.

FOR LIME BUTTER: Heat a small skillet, place 2 oz. butter in the skillet. Add the juice of ½ lime. Add chives. Pour over the crab cakes. Makes 2 cakes.

*Genie Smith*
*PLATEAU CAFE, Fredericksburg*

# Crabmeat Casserole

2 egg yolks
1 cup grated cheese
2 Tbsp. melted butter
2 cups crab meat
1/4 cup Ritz cracker crumbs
2 cups white sauce

Add cheese to hot white sauce. Stir until melted. Remove from heat. Add beaten egg yolks and crab meat. Turn into casserole. Mix butter and cracker crumbs together and sprinkle on top. Bake in 350 degree oven for 30 minutes.

*Lady Bird Johnson*

# Crawfish Etoufee

2 lbs. cleaned crawfish tails
1 stick butter, or margarine
5 medium sized onions, chopped
1/2 cup bell pepper chopped
1/2 cup celery chopped
1 Tbsp. cornstarch
2 cups water
2 tsp. tomato paste

Season crawfish tails with salt and pepper to taste. Melt butter and add onions, bell pepper and celery. Cook until well wilted. Add tomato paste and cook 20 minutes. Dissolve cornstarch in one cup water and add to mixture and cook 5 minutes. Add crawfish with one cup of water, cook 25 minutes on medium heat. Serve with rice. (For the best results use exact measures.)

*Frank Klein*

# Fish Fillets Veracruz

| | |
|---|---|
| 2 lbs. fish fillets | 1/4 tsp. oregano |
| 2 lbs. fresh tomatoes | 12 pitted green olives, |
| 2 Tbsp. lime juice | quartered |
| 2 or 3 large garlic | 2 pickled jalapeño, |
| cloves | seeded, cut in |
| 1 medium onion | strips |
| 1 large bay leaf | 1/4 cup olive oil |

Cut tomatoes in half at equator and squeeze out seeds. Chop tomatoes. Heat oil in a large skillet, add garlic (peeled and sliced) and onion; brown until soft. Add bay leaf, oregano, olives, jalapeños and tomatoes. Cook sauce over brisk flame until well seasoned and some of the juice has evaporated (about 10 min. or more if you like the sauce more reduced). This sauce can be made up to 24 hours ahead and refrigerated. Place fillets in a baking dish large enough for a single layer of fish. Pour sauce over fillets. Sprinkle an additional 3 Tbsp. of oil, if desired. Bake at 325 degrees oven 20 min. Baste fish several times while baking. Serves 4.

*Susan Muncey*

# Fried Fish Tempura

| | |
|---|---|
| 4 fillets | Salt & pepper |
| 1/2 cup flour | 1 egg white, beaten |
| 3/4 cup water | well |
| 3 Tbsp. oil | |

Make paste with flour and water, add oil, salt and pepper. Fold in beaten egg white. Pat fillet dry and lightly flour, dip in batter, fry in oil until golden brown.

*Christina Straka*

# Oysters Arachnnaise

36 large oysters, raw and drained
1 Tbsp. butter
3 Tbsp. green onion, minced
2 Tbsp. capers, minced
2 Tbsp. chives, minced
1 Tbsp. lemon juice
2 Tbsp. celery with leaves, minced
3 drops Tabasco
1½ Tbsp. butter
1 Tbsp. parsley, chopped
1 Tbsp. bell pepper, chopped
1 clove garlic, crushed
Salt, cayenne, and nutmeg, a pinch each
2 Tbsp. flour
1 cup heavy cream

Sauté oysters in a skillet, turning with 1 Tbsp. butter, green onion, capers, chives, lemon juice, celery, Tabasco. Cover and simmer gently 3 minutes, no longer. Remove from heat.

Melt 1½ Tbsp. butter in another skillet, add parsley, green pepper and simmer gently until tender. Season with salt, garlic, cayenne and nutmeg. Stir in flour until smooth, add heavy cream. Stirring constantly, heat until sauce is thickened. Pour over oysters and heat through. Serve over pasta or toast immediately.

*Johnell Livesay*

# Paella

| | |
|---|---|
| 2¹/₂ lb. frying chicken or 2 lbs. chicken breasts | 1 large tomato, peeled and coarsely chopped |
| 2¹/₂ lbs. fresh (or frozen) shrimp in their shells | 1 10 oz. pkg. frozen peas |
| 2 large cans mussels in their shells | 2¹/₂ tsp. salt |
| 1 large onion, chopped fine | 1¹/₂ tsp. saffron |
| 2 garlic cloves | 1 tsp. paprika |
| 2 cups long-grain rice, washed and drained | 2 oz. jar pimientos |
| | 1¹/₂ cups olive oil |
| | 4¹/₂ cups chicken broth |

In a skillet, sauté the chicken in 1/2 cup olive oil until it is golden brown. Remove the chicken from the skillet and reserve it. Shell and devein large shrimp and sauté them in the remaining oil in the skillet, stirring frequently, until they are pink, remove the shrimp from the skillet and reserve them.

Pour the remaining cup of olive oil into the skillet. Add the garlic and when the oil is hot, add the 2 cups of rice and cook to a golden brown. Discard garlic when it is brown. Transfer the rice to a Paella pan, or casserole. Arrange over the rice as evenly as possible the chicken pieces and the shrimp, the onions and tomato and the pkg. of frozen peas.

Bring the chicken broth to a boil and stir in the salt, saffron and paprika. Pour the hot liquid over the rice mixture in the Paella pan or casserole. Loosely cover with a sheet of aluminum foil and bake the Paella in a moderate oven 350 degree for 25 to 30 minutes, or until liquid is absorbed. Arrange the mussels in their shells, on top and arrange the pimientos, drained and cut into strips, over the surface of the dish before removing it from the heat. Garnish the dish with lemon wedges or olives and serve immediately. Serves 6.

*Elena Smith*

# Pasta Seafood Salad

1 lb. pasta shells
2 lbs. fresh shrimp
1 medium onion,
   chopped
1 10 oz. pkg. frozen
   peas
5 stalks celery,
   chopped
1 cup mayonnaise
1 cup champagne
   mustard
Dill weed to taste

Cook pasta as directed. Drain and mix with 1 Tbsp. mayonnaise. Cook peas al dente (not mushy). Chop onions and celery. Cook shrimp; peel and devein. Mix all together with rest of mayonnaise and mustard. Chill.

*Ann Mills*

# Picante Fillets

*(It's Hot, It's Good, It's Texas!)*

1¹/₂ lbs. fish fillets
1 jar (1 lb., 8 oz.) mild
   or medium picante
   sauce
2 Tbsp. canola oil
2 cups hot, cooked
   rice

Rinse fillets and cut into serving size portions. Heat oil in skillet and sear fish on both sides. Add the Picante Sauce and simmer fish for 5 to 7 minutes. Serve over hot rice. Makes 6 servings.

*Jeanine Smith*

# Poached Whole Fish

2 or 3 lb. red snapper, bass or other firm white fish (remove head if too long for pan)
1 3 oz. pkg. crab and shrimp boil
1/4 cup chopped celery
1/4 cup chopped onion
1/4 cup chopped green bell pepper
1/8 tsp. salt
3 or 4 slices of lemon

Clean and scale fish. Place crab boil and lemon slices in fish poacher or large skillet, pour in water 3 inches deep and bring to boil. Combine celery, onion, green pepper and salt; fill fish cavity. Wrap fish in cheese cloth and tie with string (can be done without the cheese cloth if fish is tied closed.) Place in the boiling water, cover, reduce heat and simmer 20 minutes or until fish flakes easily with fork. Remove fish from poacher, unwrap and enjoy. Serves 3 to 4. (This can be used in casseroles as a crab meat substitute.)

*Annabel Kellersberger*

# Salmon Burgers (Croquettes)

1 16 oz. can salmon
1 egg, slightly beaten
1 cup bread crumbs
1/2 cup chopped scallions
Salt and pepper
3 Tbsp. butter
Sour cream
1 bunch scallions

Drain salmon, reserving liquid. With fork, break salmon into small pieces. Stir beaten egg, bread crumbs and chopped scallions. Add salt and pepper to taste. (The salmon will be fairly salty, so be conservative with salt.) Mixture should be easy to shape into patties. If too dry, moisten with some of the reserved salmon liquid. Shape mixture into 6 equal-size patties. Heat butter in skillet large enough to hold six patties without crowding. When butter begins to sizzle add patties and brown well on both sides. Serve with sour cream and additional scallions and, if desired, lemon wedges. Makes 6 servings.

*Martha Kipcak*

# Sautéed Salmon

1 1/2 pounds salmon steaks or fillets
2 Tbsp. butter
1 fresh tomato coarsely chopped
1/2 cup sliced mushrooms
1 tsp. of basil or dill (fresh or dried)
1/4 tsp. (or more) garlic powder
Salt and pepper to taste

Sauté salmon in butter 5 or 6 minutes over medium heat. Turn fish over and add rest of the ingredients. Cook covered 5 or 6 minutes until fish begins to flake. Serves 4.

*Barbara Vaughan Smith*

# Shrimp Creole

2 Tbsp. oil (may need a little more)
1 large onion, chopped
1 green pepper chopped fine
4 stalks celery, chopped
2 cloves garlic minced
1 can whole tomatoes crushed
1 small can tomato sauce
5 bay leaves
Salt & pepper to taste
2 lbs. shrimp, shelled
4 Tbsp. parsley
2 green onion tops
Cayenne pepper (optional)

Fry onions, bell pepper, celery and garlic in oil until soft. Add tomatoes and sauce and cook until oil begins to bubble up over the top. Add shrimp and cook for 10 minutes. Add 3 cups water and bay leaves, cayenne, salt, and pepper. Let simmer slowly until it reaches consistency of a medium sauce. Add parsley and green onion tops. Cook a few minutes more. Serve over rice with a green salad and crispy French bread.

*Jeannine Miller*

*Variation: Add 3/4 cup sliced okra, 1/8 tsp. ground cloves and a dash of thyme to tomatoes.*

*Jan Peterson*

# Shrimp And Chicken Supreme

| | |
|---|---|
| 1 lb. medium size shrimp | 1 8 oz. pkg. cream cheese, cubed |
| 4 chicken breast halves (skinned) | 2 Tbsp. margarine |
| 1/4 tsp. garlic powder | 2 Tbsp. parmesan cheese |
| 1/4 tsp. pepper | 1 can mushroom soup |
| 2 Tbsp. margarine | 1 can celery soup, undiluted |
| 1/2 cup dry white wine | 1/2 cup bread crumbs |
| 2 10 oz. pkgs. spinach, chopped | |

The above can be made ahead and refrigerated, eliminating bread crumbs. Peel and devein shrimp. Sprinkle chicken with garlic powder and pepper. Melt 2 Tbsp. margarine in large skillet, add chicken breasts and brown lightly. Pour in wine and simmer 5 or more minutes. Remove chicken. Add shrimp to sauce in skillet and cook until pink, stirring often. Remove shrimp, reserve juices. Cook spinach according to directions (omitting salt). Drain in colander and pat dry between paper towels. Melt margarine in heavy 2 qt. sauce pan, add cream cheese, stir until smooth, add skillet juices. Add soups and blend. Cut chicken into bite size bits, add chicken, shrimp, and spinach. Stir in parmesan cheese. Spoon into greased 12"x8"x2" baking dish, sprinkle with bread crumbs. Bake 35 to 40 minutes at 350 degrees.

Serves 6 to 8.

*Nancy Kimbrell*

# Shrimp Etoufee

2 lbs. shrimp, peeled
3 Tbsp. oil
1 cup onions, chopped
1/2 cup celery, chopped
1/2 cup bell pepper
   chopped

4 cloves garlic pressed
1 Tbsp. cornstarch
2 cups water (or
   shrimp stock)
Salt, pepper, and
   cayenne to taste

Split shrimp and season (cayenne is very hot). Set aside. Sauté onions, celery and bell pepper and garlic in oil in heavy skillet, until onions are wilted. Add shrimp and let simmer, stirring occasionally for about 20 minutes. Dissolve cornstarch in water and add to mixture. Cook slowly another 15 to 20 minutes. Serve over rice. You can make shrimp stock by boiling shrimp shells in water with a bay leaf, onion and a few drops of tabasco. Drain and use for water in recipe.

*Jeannine Miller*

*Variation: 3 tsp. of tomato paste sautéed with vegetables. 1 cup chopped parsley and 1/2 cup green onion tops added 5 minutes before etoufee is done.*

*Rose Klein*

# Shrimp Irving

2 lbs. deveined shrimp
1/2 lb. butter (a must)
1/2 cup each of
   chopped green
   onions, celery, bell
   pepper, and parsley

3 garlic buds, chopped
   fine
1/2 cup dry sherry

Sauté chopped vegetables in butter. Add shrimp and cook 4 minutes or until tender. Add sherry and simmer 1 minute. Makes 4 servings. Serve on rice.

*Gretchen McWilliams*

# Shrimp Italian

12 to 14 medium shrimp, shelled and deveined
1 cup half and half cream
1 egg yolk
4 oz. butter (1 stick)
2 cloves garlic, minced
Juice of half a lemon
1 tsp. chopped fresh parsley
1 tsp. minced chives
3/4 cup flour
3/4 cup oil

Soak shrimp in half and half cream for 10 minutes. Mix yolk and lemon juice in heavy saucepan. Add 1/2 the butter, stirring until melted. Add garlic and the rest of the butter. Stir briskly until butter melts and sauce thickens. Add parsley and chives. Drain shrimp and dredge in flour. Sauté on one side only in oil over medium heat 5 minutes. DO NOT TURN. Remove from skillet, place on shallow pan and put in pre-heated broiler. Broil 5 minutes. Divide shrimp onto two warm plates and pour sauce over them. Serve with a salad and some good Italian bread to sop up this divine sauce. This is to die for! Serves 2.

*Elena Miller*

# Shrimp And Pasta Salad

2 cups shrimp boiled, cleaned and cut up*
1 12 oz. pkg. small seashell macaroni, cooked
4 green onions, sliced lengthwise and then chopped
2 stalks celery, chopped
1/2 cup chopped green olives
1/4 cup chopped green bell pepper

Mix all in a large bowl, moisten with mayonnaise and a little olive juice. Chill several hours. (I also put a few drops of Louisiana hot sauce in the mixture. You can use Tabasco). The shrimp are tasty if you boil them with some pickling spices and bay leaves or a little Tabasco in the water.

*Cocktail shrimp are good for this recipe.

*Jeannine Miller*

# Shrimp Salad Mold

1 can tomato soup
1 pkg. unflavored
    gelatin
$1/4$ cup water
1 8 oz. pkg. cream
    cheese, chopped
$1/2$ cup green pepper,
    chopped
$1/2$ cup celery,
    chopped
$1/2$ cup onion, chopped
Mayonnaise, about
    $1/2$ cup
2 lbs. boiled shrimp,
    shelled and
    deveined

Heat soup to boiling. Dissolve gelatin in water and add to soup. Add cheese. Beat with rotary beater until smooth. Add mayonnaise and mix well. Pour over chopped vegetables and shrimp. Chill. Great for luncheons.

*Denise Gruy*

# Spicy Broiled Fish

2 lbs. fish fillets
$1/4$ cup butter
6 Tbsp. champagne
    mustard
$1/2$ cup dry white wine
Lemon and dill
    seasoning

Melt butter, place fish in a foil lined pan. Baste fish with mustard. Broil 4 inches from the heat for 5 minutes. Sprinkle lemon and dill seasoning on top. Pour wine over fish and broil about 5 minutes or until fish flakes.

*Ann Mills*

*How to run your life:*

> *Cry when things are sad.*
> *Laugh when things are funny.*
> *Pray when things are scary.*
> *Give thanks when things are good.*

# Shrimp And Squash Casserole

*(A Crowd Pleaser)*

| | |
|---|---|
| 1 1/2 lbs. yellow squash (3 cups yellow squash) | 1/2 cup whipping cream or small can chilled milk |
| 3/4 cup raw shrimp | 1 Tbsp. instant minced onion |
| 2 Tbsp. butter | 1/2 cup coarse bread crumbs |
| 2 Tbsp. flour | 1/4 cup grated parmesan cheese |
| 1/2 tsp. salt | 1 Tbsp. butter |
| 1/8 tsp. black pepper | |
| 1 cup chicken broth (use bouillon cube) | |

Wash and dry squash. Cut crosswise into 1/4 inch slices. Thoroughly rinse shrimp under cold water. Drain. Heat the butter in sauce pan. Blend in flour, salt and pepper. Cook until it bubbles. Remove from heat and add chicken broth gradually stirring constantly. Bring to boil for 1 or 2 minutes. Blend in cream and minced onions. Mix in the raw shrimp. Put in layer of squash in bottom of a 1 1/2 qt. casserole and spoon half of the shrimp sauce over squash. Repeat layer with remaining squash and shrimp sauce. Cover tightly and set in a 400 degree oven for 30 minutes. Meanwhile, toss crumbs and parmesan cheese with melted butter. After 30 minutes remove casserole from oven and reduce heat to 350 degrees. Remove cover and top with bread crumbs. Return to oven 15 minutes or until crumbs are golden brown.

*Lady Bird Johnson*

*THE L.B.J. COMPLEX*                                              1983

From the collection of
Leo and Anyta Jones, Tyler, Texas

Lady Bird Johnson, wife of the late president, Lyndon B. Johnson, has been a member of
St. Barnabas Episcopal Church since pre-White House days. Their lovely ranch is a popular
tourist attraction twelve miles east of Fredericksburg. Look for Mrs. Johnson's recipes throughout the cookbook.

# Asparagus Parmesan

1½ lbs. asparagus, cleaned and trimmed
3 Tbsp. lightly salted butter
½ cup mayonnaise
⅛ tsp. dry mustard
¼ cup freshly squeezed lemon juice
½ cup fresh bread crumbs
⅓ cup grated Parmesan cheese
1 Tbsp. chopped fresh parsley

Preheat oven to 350 degrees. Butter oblong casserole. Steam asparagus 3 minutes. Place in pan. Lightly brown 2 Tbsp. butter, mix with mayonnaise, mustard, and lemon juice; pour over asparagus. Melt remaining 1 Tbsp. butter and toss with bread crumbs. Sprinkle asparagus with bread crumbs, cheese, and parsley. Bake 15 to 20 minutes until lightly browned.

*Doris Smith*

# Bitsy's Broccoli

2 10 oz. pkgs. frozen chopped broccoli
4 slices of bread, made into crumbs
½ cup melted butter
½ cup slivered almonds
1 6 oz. tube garlic cheese
½ small onion, chopped

Cook broccoli and drain well. Add tube of cheese and stir until it is melted. Sauté crumbs, onion, and almonds in the melted butter until golden. Add sautéed mixture to broccoli and cheese. Pour into a lightly buttered casserole and sprinkle with additional bread crumbs and almonds. Bake at 350 degrees for 20 minutes. Serves 6.

*Karen Benignus Laurence*

# Green Beans
# With Garlic Butter

| | |
|---|---|
| 1/4 cup sliced almonds | 1 16 oz. can green |
| 2 Tbsp. butter | beans or fresh |
| 1 clove garlic minced | beans or fresh |
| | cooked |

Toss almonds with butter and garlic in skillet until butter is melted, add beans, heat thoroughly over medium fire.

*Pearl Herbort*

# Broccoli Continental

| | |
|---|---|
| 2 10 oz. pkgs. chopped | 1/2 cup chopped celery |
| broccoli | 1 can cream of |
| 1 stick margarine | mushroom soup |
| 1 can drained | 1 roll garlic flavored |
| mushrooms | cheese |
| 1 bunch shallots | |

Sauté shallots, mushrooms and celery in margarine. Melt cheese roll with mushroom soup. Partially cook broccoli and drain well. Mix all ingredients and pour into greased casserole and bake at 350 degrees for 20 minutes.

*This is my son Noel's favorite dish.*

*Bobby Sawatzky*

# Frijoles Negros (Black Beans)

**BEANS:**
1 lb. black turtle beans
1 medium white onion
   (coarsely sliced)
$^1/_2$ head of garlic,
   peeled
10 cups hot water
2 tsp. salt
2 stems epazote

**SALSA ROJA:**
2 small tomatoes
3 serrano chilies
2 garlic cloves
$^1/_4$ onion, chopped
1 Tbsp. vegetable oil
Salt to taste

**GARNISHES:**
6 green onions,
   chopped
Lime wedges,
   quartered
2 tomatoes, chopped
2 fresh jalapeños,
   chopped
$^1/_2$ cup cilantro,
   chopped

Beans: Pick beans, rinse in cold water, drain; repeat. Put beans in bean pot or large casserole (preferably cast iron). Add onion and garlic, cover with hot water. Cover and cook over medium heat until beans are soft, anywhere from 4-8 hours, depending on the age of the beans. Add salt and epazote to taste. Cook approximately 30 minutes longer. Serve garnishes separately to be added to beans as desired.

Salsa Roja (Red Sauce): Roast chilies on griddle over medium heat until blistered on all sides. Cut off stems. Cut tomatoes in half and remove hard core. Put roasted chilies, tomatoes, onion and garlic in blender and process until puréed. Heat oil in saucepan over moderate heat, add chilie mixture and bring to a boil. Add salt to taste. Always cook beans one day in advance so the flavors develop.

*Denise Miller Gruy*

# Party Walnut Broccoli

| | |
|---|---|
| 3 10 oz. pkgs. frozen chopped broccoli | ²/₃ cup water |
| 6 Tbsp. margarine | 2 cups herb poultry stuffing (crumbly type) |
| 4 Tbsp. flour | ²/₃ cup chopped walnuts |
| 1 cup chicken broth | |
| 2 cups skim milk | |

Cook broccoli according to package directions until just barely tender. Drain well and place in oiled 2 quart casserole. Melt 2 Tbsp. margarine in saucepan. Stir in flour, cook briefly, add milk. Add chicken broth and cook, stirring constantly until thickened. Set aside.

Melt remaining 4 Tbsp. margarine in ²/₃ cup water. Mix with herb dressing and walnuts. Pour chicken broth over broccoli, sprinkle evenly with walnut mixture and bake at 400 degrees for 20 minutes or until crusty on top.

*Mary Lindsey*

# Herbed Brussels Sprouts

| | |
|---|---|
| 8 cups brussels sprouts | 3 Tbsp. dijon mustard |
| ³/₄ cup chicken stock | 1 cup heavy cream |
| ¹/₄ cup white wine | ¹/₄ to ¹/₂ cup toasted, slivered almonds |
| ¹/₄ tsp. dried sage | |

Simmer brussels sprouts in stock and wine 10 to 12 minutes, until barely tender. Drain all but 2 Tbsp. stock mixture. Stir in sage, mustard, and cream. Shake pan to coat sprouts. Sprinkle with almonds.

*Doris Smith*

# Skillet Cabbage

| | |
|---|---|
| 2 pieces bacon | 4 to 5 slices American processed cheese |
| ¹/₂ head cabbage, shredded | Pepper, to taste |
| 1 onion, shredded | Sugar, sprinkle |

Fry bacon, drain, crumble, and set aside. Sauté cabbage and onion until limp. Add pepper, sugar, and cheese slices. Cook about 5 minutes stirring several times. Add crumbled bacon on top.

*C.C. Gibbons*

# Glazed Carrots

*(No Fat)*

3/4 cup water
8 medium carrots,
   peeled, sliced
   1/4" thick
1 stick cinnamon
3/4 tsp. ground cumin
1/2 tsp. ground ginger

1/2 tsp. ground
   coriander
1/8 tsp. cayenne
   pepper
2 tsp. honey
2 tsp. lemon juice

In 10 inch skillet bring water to boil. Add carrots, cinnamon, cumin, ginger, coriander, and pepper. Cover, gently simmer 12 minutes. Uncover, add honey and lemon juice. Heat to high until liquid evaporates and carrots are tender.

*Delores Sinks*

# Carrot And Zucchini Pancakes

*(A Surprise Treat)*

1 cup grated carrots
1/2 cup grated zucchini
2 scallions, sliced
1/2 cup flour

1/2 tsp. baking powder
1/2 tsp. salt
1 egg
1/4 cup milk

Mix carrots, zucchini and scallions together. Mix flour, baking powder and salt together. Mix milk and egg together and stir into dry ingredients, add this to carrot and zucchini mixture. Drop by tablespoons onto hot griddle or skillet, cooking until golden on each side.

*Micki George*

# Lemon-Butter Cauliflower

8 cups cauliflower florets
Juice of half a lemon
2 Tbsp. capers, rinsed and drained
1 Tbsp. chopped, fresh parsley for garnish
1 Tbsp. chopped chives for garnish
¹/₃ cup freshly squeezed lemon juice
¹/₄ cup lightly salted butter

Boil florets with juice of half lemon in water 10 to 15 minutes until tender. Melt butter; stir in lemon juice and capers. Pour over cauliflower. Sprinkle with parsley and chives.

*Doris Smith*

# Celery Amandine

4 cups diagonally sliced celery
¹/₄ plus 2 Tbsp. butter or margarine
Salt and pepper to taste
2 Tbsp. chives, finely chopped
2 Tbsp. onions, grated
1 clove garlic, crushed
2 Tbsp. dry white wine
¹/₂ to 1 cup slivered almonds

Sauté celery in ¹/₄ cup butter, stirring occasionally. Add next 5 ingredients. Cover and cook over low heat about 10 minutes, until celery is tender. Sauté almonds in remaining butter; add to celery, and cook 1 additional minute. 4 to 5 servings.

*Nancy Wareing*

# Creole Corn And Tomatoes

2 slices bacon
1 large onion, chopped
1 medium green
    pepper, chopped
1 can tomatoes,
    crushed
1 can creamed style
    corn
$1/4$ tsp. salt
$1/4$ tsp. pepper
1 bay leaf, optional

Fry bacon, remove from skillet. Add onion and bell pepper. Cook until translucent, add tomatoes and seasonings. Cook down and then add corn. Cook about 10 minutes on low fire.

*Mildred Roper*

# Donna Booe's Corn Casserole

1 16 oz. can creamed
    corn
1 cup evaporated milk
$1/2$ cup fine cracker
    crumbs, saltines
3 eggs, beaten
1 medium onion,
    chopped
$1/4$ tsp. salt
$1/8$ tsp. pepper
$1 1/2$ cups shredded
    sharp cheddar
    cheese

Combine corn, milk, cracker crumbs, eggs, onions, salt and pepper in a mixing bowl. Place $1/2$ of above mixture in 8 inch square pyrex baking dish. Top with $1/2$ of shredded cheese. Layer remaining mixture and top with cheese again. Bake in preheated oven at 350 degrees for 35 minutes. Serves 6 to 8.

*Virginia Muncey*

# Texas Corn Casserole

| | |
|---|---|
| 1 17 oz. can creamed corn | 1/2 cup chopped green bell pepper |
| 1 17 oz. can whole kernel corn, drained | 1 egg, beaten |
| 1 cup grated sharp cheddar cheese | 2/3 cup evaporated milk |
| 1 1/3 cups seasoned bread crumbs | 4 Tbsp. butter, melted |
| 1/2 cup grated onion | 1 tsp. salt |
| 1/2 cup chopped red bell pepper | 1 1/2 tsp. pepper |
| | 1/2 tsp. cayenne pepper |

Reserve 1/3 cup of bread crumbs for topping. Mix remaining ingredients together and stir well. Pour into slightly greased casserole and sprinkle with reserved crumbs and paprika. Bake at 400 degrees 45-55 minutes. Serves 10 to 12.

*Karen B. Laurence*

# Eggplant Dressing

| | |
|---|---|
| 1 large peeled and diced eggplant (4 cups) | 1 pkg. herb seasoned stuffing mix |
| 1 can mushroom soup | 2 Tbsp. melted margarine |
| 1/3 cup milk | 1 cup shredded cheddar |
| 1 beaten egg | |
| 1/2 cup chopped onion | |

Cook diced eggplant in salted boiling water 6 to 7 minutes or until tender. Drain. Stir milk into soup. Blend in egg. Add eggplant, onion, and stuffing, reserving 1/2 to 3/4 cup stuffing. Toss lightly to mix. Turn into 10"x6"x1 1/2" greased dish. Toss remaining stuffing with melted margarine. Sprinkle over casserole. Top with cheddar. Bake at 350 degrees for 20 minutes. Serves 6 to 8.

*Betty R. Robinson*

# Eggplant With Pesto

*(Microwave)*

2 small eggplant, cut
  in half
1 tsp. salt

$^1/_2$ tsp. pepper
1 Tbsp. olive oil

Score halved eggplant, sprinkle with salt. Rinse and let drain at least $^1/_2$ hour. Put halves drizzled with olive oil, salt and pepper in microwave. Cook for 6 minutes or until soft.

**PESTO:**
2 cups fresh basil, no
  stems, lightly
  packed
6 cloves garlic

1 cup parmesan
  cheese
1 cup olive oil
1$^1/_2$ cups any kind of
  nuts

Mix pesto ingredients together, whirl in blender. Make a sandwich with pesto between eggplant halves or serve open with pesto spread on top of each.

*Catherine Joseffy*

# Fideo

7 or 8 Vermicelli coils
2 or 3 garlic cloves,
  sliced
$^1/_2$ cup oil
1 cup chopped onion
1 15 oz. can tomatoes
$^1/_2$ tsp. dried oregano

$^1/_2$ tsp. ground
  cominos
2$^1/_2$ cups chicken
  broth (water can be
  used)
1 tsp. salt and $^1/_2$ tsp.
  pepper, or to taste

Pour oil into a heavy skillet large enough to hold vermicelli in single layer. Put in garlic and vermicelli and lightly brown vermicelli on both sides leaving the coils in tact. Drain off excess oil. Add onion, tomatoes with juice, oregano, cominos, salt and pepper. Add broth or water or enough to cover vermicelli and bring to a boil. Reduce heat to low. Cover and cook until vermicelli is done, about 20 minutes, and water is mostly absorbed. Do not stir while cooking. This is a delicious side dish. Serves 6-8.

*Elena Smith*

## Cheese Grits

6 cups boiling water
1 1/2 cups grits
1 lb. velveeta cheese
1/2 lb. butter or margarine
2 tsp. seasoned salt
Dash Tabasco, to taste
3 eggs, beaten

Add grits to boiling water, cook 4-5 minutes. Add to hot grits the rest of ingredients. Bake 1 hour at 350 degrees 9"x13" casserole. Serves 10-12.

*Gloria Hall*

## Fettuccine Alla Romana

1/3 cup whipped butter
3 cloves garlic, crushed
2 Tbsp. minced prosciutto ham
1/3 cup cooked green peas
1/2 cup heavy cream
1/2 lb. fettuccine noodles, al dente
1 egg, slightly beaten
4 Tbsp. freshly grated parmesan cheese

Melt butter slowly in wok or saucepan and add garlic. As butter bubbles, add prosciutto, and peas. Add cream. Add pasta, egg, and cheese, tossing gently with 2 large spoons until cheese is melted. Serves 2-4.

*Ann Mills*

## Linguine With Fresh Tomato Sauce

3 lbs. very ripe tomatoes, coarsely chopped, liquid reserved.
1 lb. linguine
1/2 cup coarsely chopped fresh basil
3 Tbsp. red wine vinegar
4 Tbsp. olive oil
2 Tbsp. minced garlic
Salt and freshly ground pepper to taste
1 Tbsp. extra virgin olive oil
Freshly grated parmesan cheese

Heat 1 Tbsp. oil in small skillet. Add garlic and stir about 3 minutes, do not brown. Transfer to non-aluminum bowl. Mix in tomatoes and liquid. Season with salt and pepper. Let stand 6 hours. Just before serving, cook linguine until tender but still firm. Drain and transfer to large bowl. Add sauce and toss. Pass parmesan cheese.

*Linda Zehnder*

# 1015 Onion Casserole

| | |
|---|---|
| 1/2 cup butter | 1 tsp. salt |
| 7 large 1015 onions | 2 cups slivered sharp |
| 1/2 cup rice | cheese |
| 5 cups boiling water | 2/3 cup half and half |

Slice onions and sauté in butter until soft. In another pot cook rice in boiling, salted water for 8 minutes. Drain well. Blend rice with onions, cheese and cream. Place in greased casserole. Bake about an hour at 325 degrees. This dish travels well, as it is still tasty at room temperature.

*Mary Ann Smith*

# Spaghetti With Garlic And Oil

| | |
|---|---|
| 1/2 cup plus 1 Tbsp. olive oil | Freshly ground pepper, 6-8 twists of the mill |
| 2 tsp. very finely chopped garlic | 2 Tbsp. chopped parsley |
| 2 tsp. salt | |
| 1 lb. spaghetti or spaghettini | |

Heat water in a large pot for the spaghetti. In a small saucepan sauté 1/2 cup oil, garlic and salt over very low heat, stirring frequently, until it slowly becomes a rich, golden color.

Drop the spaghetti into the boiling water and cook until barely tender, very firm to the bite. Drain immediately, transfer to a warm bowl, and add the garlic and oil sauce. Toss rapidly, coating all strands, adding pepper and parsley. Mix the remaining tablespoon of olive oil into the spaghetti and serve. This is one of the easiest, quickest and tastiest pasta dishes you can prepare. Great for last minute meals.

*Diane Matthews*

# Rolled Manicotti

1/2 cup olive oil
1 cup chopped onions
6 large cloves garlic
minced
2 15 oz. cans peeled
tomatoes
2 6 oz. cans tomato
paste
1 cup Burgundy Wine
1 tsp. salt
1/8 tsp. pepper
2 tsp. sugar
4 Tbsp. chopped
parsley
4 Tbsps. basil
1 tsp. oregano

1/4 tsp. cloves
1/4 tsp. nutmeg
1 tsp. minced
anchovies or
anchovy paste
2 pints Ricotta cheese
1 lb. monterey jack
cheese, grated
1 lb. mozzarella
cheese, grated
4 eggs
1/2 cup parmesan
cheese
1 Tbsp. parsley
2 large pkgs. lasagne
noodles

Put olive oil in 4 quart sauce pan and place over low heat, 250 degrees. Sauté onions and garlic until they are tender and clear. Add tomatoes, tomato paste, Burgundy Wine, salt, pepper, sugar, parsley, basil, oregano, cloves, nutmeg, and anchovies or anchovy paste.

In large bowl, place Ricotta cheese, monterey jack, mozzarella, parmesan and parsley. Beat in eggs one at a time until smooth. Set aside. Bring water and 1 Tbsp. salt to a boil in large pot (2 gallon). Add noodles one at a time. Cook until tender around 10 minutes. Drain. Place in cool water.

Take one drained noodle and place on cookie sheet. Spread cheese mixture on noodle. Roll up noodle and cheese. In large pan around 10"x13"x3", cover bottom with sauce. Place rolled noodle, flat down, in pan. Continue until all noodles are used. Cover noodles with rest of the sauce. Bake in oven at 350 degrees for 30 minutes. Remove from oven. Let set for 20 minutes. Serve warm.

*Jean Wieser*

# Buffet Pasta

**10-12 oz. spaghetti**
**1 cup (more or less)**
**grated parmesan**
**cheese**

**6 oz. butter**

Cook spaghetti (10 or 12 oz.) as usual, when done, drain and soak in cold water 30 min. Drain WELL, dust thoroughly with parmesan cheese. Place on deep platter. Right before serving, brown butter in small skillet (but Don't Burn!) pour over pasta. This can be served at room temperature or warmed in oven.

*Alethia Alt*

# Green Peas With Garlic And Dill Weed

**1 16 oz. pkg. frozen**
**green peas**
**1/2 cup onion, chopped**
**fine**
**2 stalks celery,**
**chopped fine**

**1/2 red pepper,**
**chopped fine**
**1 tsp. garlic powder**
**1/2 tsp. dill weed**
**2 Tbsp. margarine**
**3/4 cup water**

Bring water to boil in saucepan. Add peas, onion, and celery, bring to a second boil. Stir, cover, and reduce heat. Simmer 6 minutes or to desired tenderness. Drain water from peas, then add chopped red pepper, margarine, garlic and dill. Let sit a few minutes before serving.

*Doris Smith*

# Willie's Black Eyed Peas

*(My Father-In-Law's Favorite Recipe)*

| | |
|---|---|
| 2 11 oz. pkgs. fresh shelled black-eyed peas | 1 tsp. bouquet garni |
| 1 16 oz. pkg. frozen field peas | 3 tsp. tarragon vinegar |
| 1 green pepper, chopped | ¹/₂ tsp. salt |
| 1 white onion, minced | 4 tsp. sugar |
| 6 strips thick-sliced bacon, finely chopped | ¹/₂ tsp. garlic powder |
| 2 stalks celery, including tops, finely sliced | ¹/₂ can chopped green chilies |
| 1 tsp. coarse ground pepper | ¹/₂ 2 oz. jar chopped pimientos |
| | 1 cube Knorr's chicken bouillon |
| | 2 cans Chicken Broth (or 20 oz. homemade) |
| | 2 cups water |

Use 3 qt. sauce pan. Cook bacon, chopped, until well done. Drain. Add green pepper, onion, celery, pepper, salt, Bouquet Garni, garlic powder and sauté until tender. Add chicken broth, water and all other ingredients and bring to a boil. Reduce heat, cover and simmer 1¹/₂ hours.

*Gwen Kinney*

# Potato Puff

*(A favorite recipe of my Mothers that I enjoyed as a gift and continue to enjoy today.)*

| | |
|---|---|
| 8 medium potatoes, | 2 well beaten egg whites |
| 2 well beaten egg yolks | Salt and pepper to taste |
| salt and pepper to taste | |
| 1 heaping Tbsp. butter | |
| ¹/₂ cup heated milk | |

Cook, drain and mash potatoes thoroughly. Add salt, pepper, butter and heated milk. Whip into potatoes. Beat in egg yolks, then fold in the egg whites. Place into greased casserole. Bake at 350 degrees for 30 minutes until puffed and brown.

*Marcella Miller*

# Garlic Mashed Potatoes

3 large baking
   potatoes, peeled
   and quartered
3 large red potatoes,
   peeled and
   quartered

8 cloves garlic, peeled
   and halved
3/4 cup low fat milk
2 Tbsp. butter
Salt and pepper to
   taste

Bring to boil the potatoes and garlic in water. Cover and cook over medium heat 30 minutes. Drain. Partly mash potatoes and garlic. Add butter and milk, mash until creamy. Stir in salt and pepper to taste.

*Delores Sinks*

# Heisser Kartoffelsalat

*(Hot Potato Salad)*

6 medium sized
   potatoes
1/4 cup finely chopped
   onion
6 strips bacon diced
1/2 cup cider vinegar

1 1/2 Tbsp. sugar
2 tsp. salt
A small amount coarse
   ground black
   pepper

Cook potatoes in boiling salted water until done. Peel and cube. Season with salt and pepper. Fry bacon until crisp and drain. Add to potatoes. Heat onion in bacon fat until partly done. Add vinegar and sugar to onion and bacon fat. Heat to boiling point. Pour over potatoes and mix lightly. Serve at once. This salad keeps well when refrigerated and is good served cold. Follow this recipe for sweet potato salad also.

*Bessie Evers*

# Jalapeño Potatoes

| | |
|---|---|
| 8 | medium new potatoes, boil unpeeled, cool and slice |
| 1 | bell pepper, chopped |
| 1 | large onion, chopped |
| $^1/_2$ cup melted butter |
| 2 | Tbsp. flour |
| 2 | cups milk |
| 10 oz. pkg. | Velveeta jalapeño cheese |
| 1 | small jar pimientos |

Preheat oven 350 degrees. Lay sliced potatoes flat in buttered 3 qt. 9"x13" pan, salt and pepper to taste. In a skillet, sauté peppers and onions in $^1/_2$ cup butter. Add flour and stir until bubbly. Add milk and cheese, stir until melted. Add pimientos. Pour over potatoes. Bake 45 minutes. (A family favorite. Good if baked the day before.) Serves 10.

*Linda Campbell*

# World's Easiest Potato Casserole

| | |
|---|---|
| 8 oz. | sour cream |
| 6 Tbsp. | butter or margarine, melted |
| 1 2 lb. bag | frozen hash brown potatoes |
| 1 can | cream of mushroom soup |
| $1^1/_2$ cups | grated cheddar cheese |
| 1 bunch | green onions, chopped |
| | Salt, fresh ground pepper to taste |
| | Garlic powder to taste |

Mix sour cream, melted butter, soup, cheese, and onions. Put potatoes in greased casserole, and pour cream mixture over. Poke a few holes in potatoes to let mixture seep in. Cover and bake 1 hour and 15 minutes at 350 degrees. Remove cover and bake 15 minutes more.

*Gwen Kinney*
*Doris Schmid*

# Smothered Okra

1/2 cup oil
1 lb. chopped okra,
   fresh or frozen
1 onion, chopped fine
1/2 cup bell pepper,
   chopped fine
3 (or more) cloves of
   garlic, minced

1 15 oz. can tomatoes
   (or 2 cups ripe,
   fresh chopped)
1 tsp. salt
1/4 tsp. cayenne
   pepper
1/4 tsp. black pepper

In heavy pot with lid smother okra in oil, covered, 15 minutes over medium low heat, stir often. Add onions, tomatoes, garlic, bell pepper, and seasoning. Simmer over low heat 30 minutes, covered stirring occasionally. Serves 4 to 5.

*Alethia Alt*

# Baked Onions

4 large or 6 medium
   onions (1015, Walla
   Walla or Vidalia)
1 Tbsp. butter or
   margarine

1 small carton
   pimiento cheese
   spread
15 to 20 Ritz
   Crackers, crushed

Sauté onions in butter, cover until limp, or microwave in casserole until limp. Cover all over with pimiento spread and crushed Ritz crackers. Heat at 325 degrees until bubbly and toasty brown.

*C.C. Gibbons*

# Buffet Rice

| | |
|---|---|
| 2 cups rice | 2 or 3 green onions, chopped with tops |
| 5 Tbsp. soy sauce | |
| 4 oz. butter | 1/2 cup toasted almonds |
| 5 beef bouillon cubes | |

In large heavy skillet sauté rice in butter until brown. Set aside. Dissolve bouillon cubes in 3$^1$/$_2$ cups of boiling water. Add to rice. Cook covered 30 minutes on low heat. Add soy sauce, almonds, green onions with tops. Cover with cup towel, steam 15 minutes over low fire. Serves 8. This holds well off stove if kept covered or can be reheated before serving.

*Angela Poen*

# Rice Casserole

| | |
|---|---|
| 2$^1$/$_2$ cups rice, uncooked | 1 4 oz. can chopped green chilies |
| 2 pkgs. sliced Monterey Jack cheese | 2 cups sour cream |
| | 1/2 cup grated cheddar cheese |

Cook rice. Grease casserole (about 9"x12"), spread half the rice in bottom, followed with a layer of half the sliced cheese, next half the green chilies and layer of half the sour cream. Repeat the process. Top with the cheddar, sour cream. Repeat the process. Top with the cheddar. Bake 30 minutes at 350 degrees. Serves 6-8.

*Mary Lois Clark*

# Toasted Rice And Pasta Pikes

1 Tbsp. oil
3/4 cup raw rice
2/3 cup spaghetti,
  broken in 1"
  lengths
1 small onion,
  chopped
1 can chicken broth or
  10 oz. of
  homemade
1/2 bay leaf
1/4 cup parsley

Heat oil in heavy skillet over medium heat. Add rice and spaghetti. Cook until golden brown 3-5 minutes. Add onion and cook 3 minutes longer. Stir to prevent scorching. Add broth and bay leaf, lower heat. Cover and cook 15-17 minutes or until broth is absorbed. Stir in parsley and fluff. Serves 4-6.

*Betty Robinson*

# Spinach Artichoke Bake

1 can artichoke halves
3 pkgs. spinach,
  cooked and drained
  dry
1/2 lb. cream cheese
2 Tbsp. mayonnaise
6 Tbsp. milk
Pepper
1/3 cup Romano and
  Parmesan cheese

Mix together cream cheese, mayonnaise and milk. Layer artichoke halves, spinach, then cream cheese mixture, sprinkle with pepper and then cheese. Bake at 375 degrees for 40 minutes.

*Jeannine Miller*
*Doris Smith*

# Summer Squash Casserole

| 2 lbs. yellow squash | 8 oz. pkg. herb |
| 1/4 cup onion, chopped | stuffing mix |
| 1 can cream of | 1/2 cup butter or |
| chicken soup | margarine |
| 1 cup sour cream | 1 tsp. salt |
| 1 cup shredded carrot | |

Combine squash, salt, and onion in saucepan. Cover in water and boil 5 minutes. Drain. Combine soup and sour cream in a bowl, stir in carrots, and fold in squash mixture. Combine stuffing mix and butter. Spread half on the bottom of a 12"x7¹/₂"x2" casserole. Spoon vegetable mixture over stuffing. Sprinkle rest of stuffing over top. Bake 25-30 minutes at 350 degrees. Serves 6.

*Esther Taylor*

# Company Sweet Potatoes

| 4 medium sweet | 1/4 tsp. cinnamon |
| potatoes | 1/4 tsp. nutmeg |
| 1/2 cup orange | 1/4 tsp. allspice |
| marmalade | 1/2 cup chopped |
| 1 tsp. butter | pecans |

Peel and grate potatoes and combine with marmalade, using enough to moisten. Put mixture in buttered (no substitutes) pyrex baking dish, sprinkle with spices. Dot with butter and cover with pecans. Bake at 350 degrees 35 to 45 minutes.

*Cay Meadows*

# Tomatoes Provençal

*(Using fresh herbs makes this dish heavenly)*

2 Tbsp. fresh bread crumbs

1/4 cup finely chopped onion

1/4 cup finely chopped fresh parsley

1/2 tsp. minced garlic

2 Tbsp. sweet butter or margarine, softened

1 Tbsp. Chopped fresh basil or 1 tsp. dried

1/2 tsp. fresh thyme or 1/4 dried

1/2 tsp. salt

1/8 tsp. freshly ground pepper

4 large tomatoes, cut in wedges

Preheat oven to 425 degrees. Grease baking dish. Mix bread crumbs with onion, parsley, garlic, butter, basil, thyme, salt and pepper. Place tomatoes in prepared baking dish. Sprinkle with herb mixture. Bake 8-10 minutes or until tomatoes are tender.

*Doris Smith*

# Tomato Pie

1 unbaked pie shell, deep

4 thick, peeled, sliced tomatoes

1 cup mayonnaise

1 cup cheddar cheese, grated

1/2 cup sliced black olives

4 leaves chopped fresh basil (dried may be used)

Layer in 3 layers, bake 35 minutes at 350 degrees.

*Ann Baker*

# Baked Cherry And Yellow Tomatoes

1 lb. cherry tomatoes, or half red half small yellow mixed
1 Tbsp. garlic minced
1 Tbsp. fresh rosemary chopped
1 tsp. salt
$^{1}/_{2}$ cup fresh grated parmesan
$^{1}/_{2}$ cup white bread crumbs (from French bread)
Fresh ground pepper to taste
$^{1}/_{2}$ to $^{3}/_{4}$ cup olive oil

Cut tomatoes in half. Place, cut side up, in large shallow baking dish, close together. Salt and pepper tomatoes well. Mix garlic and rosemary with bread crumbs and sprinkle evenly over tomatoes. Top with parmesan. Drizzle olive oil over all. Bake 40 to 45 minutes, uncovered, in 350 degree oven. A pretty dish as well as delicious.

*Johnell Livesay*

# Baked Vegetables A La Greek

4 celery stalks
2 large onions, chopped
3 zucchini, cut in 1" slices
1 can green beans
4 carrots, cut in 1" slices
2 15 oz. cans tomatoes with juice
3 or 4 potatoes peeled and cut in large pieces
3 or 4 (or more) cloves garlic sliced
2 cups cut broccoli, fresh or frozen
1 Tbsp. oregano
2 tsp. salt
$^{1}/_{2}$ tsp. pepper
$^{1}/_{2}$ cup olive oil

Put all ingredients in large greased baking pan, at least 2" deep, that has been rubbed generously with oil. Mix and drizzle over $^{1}/_{2}$ cup olive oil. Cover with foil, bake 350 degrees for $1^{1}/_{2}$-2 hours (or until carrots and potatoes are tender.) A variety of vegetables may be used, but always use tomatoes, onions, and seasonings. Cooked beef or lamb may be added to pan or ground dry beef bouillon. For less cooking time, parboil carrots and potatoes first.
Serves 8 to 10.

*Alethia Alt*

# Marinated Vegetable Platter

1 cauliflower head separated into florets
1 broccoli head separated into florets
8 oz. fresh green beans, halved
4 large carrots cut diagonally into thin strips
2 red or green bell peppers, cut into strips

MARINADE:
1/2 cup red wine vinegar
1 Tbsp. lemon juice
1 1/2 tsp. worcestershire sauce
1 tsp. sugar
1 tsp. dry mustard
2 garlic cloves, minced
1 1/2 cups peanut or vegetable oil
Salt and pepper to taste

Blanch vegetables (except peppers) separately until crisp-tender. (Can be prepared one day ahead). Mix vegetables and peppers with dressing and marinate at room temperature 1 to 4 hours. Drain vegetables and arrange on lettuce-lined platter. Sprinkle with chopped, fresh chives. Serves 8.

*Linda Zehnder*

# Italian Zucchini

2 lbs. zucchini
1/4 cup olive oil or vegetable oil
1 1/2 cup onions, sliced
1 1/2 tsp. salt
1/4 tsp. pepper
1 tsp. Italian seasoning or 1/4 tsp. oregano and thyme or basil and cumin
3 cups tomato juice or canned tomatoes, crushed

Cut zucchini in half lengthwise and then crosswise into 3 inch long pieces. Heat oil in skillet, add zucchini green side up, add onions, brown lightly on cut side over low heat. Turn cut side up: add salt, pepper, Italian spices and tomatoes or juice. Cover, cook over low heat 40 minutes or until tender and sauce is thickened.

*Jeannine Miller*

# Zucchini Pie

| | |
|---|---|
| 4 cups thinly sliced zucchini | 2 beaten eggs |
| 1 cup chopped onions | $^1/_4$ tsp. oregano |
| $^1/_2$ cup margarine | 2 cups shredded mozzarella cheese |
| 2 Tbsp. parsley flakes | 8 oz. can refrigerator quick crescent dinner rolls |
| $^1/_2$ tsp. salt | |
| $^1/_2$ tsp. pepper | 2 tsp. mustard |
| $^1/_4$ tsp. garlic powder | |
| $^1/_4$ tsp. basil | |

Cook and stir zucchini and onion in margarine for 10 minutes. Add spices. Add eggs to cheese, stir zucchini mixture into eggs and cheese. Separate dinner rolls into 8 triangles. Place in ungreased 10" pie pan, spreading over bottom and sides. Spread crust with mustard. Pour vegetable mixture into crust. Bake at 375 degrees for 18-20 minutes. Cover with foil for last 10 minutes of baking. Let stand 10 minutes. Serves 6

*Gretchen McWilliams*

*Variation: 1 cup chopped mushroom instead of onions.*

*Melissa Miller*

# Scalloped Zucchini With Sausage

3 medium zucchini
$1/4$ lb. sausage
$1/4$ cup chopped onion
$1/4$ cup finely crushed
   crackers (8)
$1/4$ cup parmesan
   cheese, grated

1 slightly beaten egg
$1/2$ tsp. salt
$1/8$ tsp. thyme
Dash garlic salt
Dash pepper
2 Tbsp. parmesan
   cheese

Scrub zucchini squash, cut off ends, cook whole in salted water until tender, about 15 minutes. Drain, reserving $1/2$ cup liquid, chop zucchini coarsely. In skillet cook sausage and onion until sausage is browned and onion is tender, drain, add squash, reserved liquid and remaining ingredients. Mix well. Turn into ungreased casserole, sprinkle with parmesan cheese. Bake at 350 degrees for 40 minutes or until set and delicately browned.

*Jeannine Miller*

# Fonda San Miguel's Calabacita Rellena

4 medium to large
  zucchini
2 cups fresh or frozen
  corn kernels (not
  canned)
2 eggs
2 Tbsp. milk (if using
  frozen corn)
$^1/_4$ tsp. salt

6 oz. mild cheddar or
  monterey jack
  cheese, grated
3 medium tomatoes
$^1/_4$ onion (more to
  taste)
1 clove garlic (more to
  taste)
$^1/_8$ tsp. salt
2 Tbsp. cooking oil

Cut zucchini in half lengthwise. Scoop out pulp leaving a $^1/_2$ inch shell. What you will have left will resemble little zucchini canoes. Put shells in an oiled baking dish and set aside. Purée the corn, eggs, milk, and salt in blender. Do not add any more milk than absolutely necessary. You should not need any if using fresh corn. Pour purée in a small bowl, add grated cheese and mix well. Spoon into the prepared zucchini. Cover pan with foil and bake for 50 minutes at 350 degrees. While the zucchini is baking, broil the whole tomatoes until the skin starts to turn black in places and they shrivel a little. Put the tomatoes, onion, and garlic in a blender or food processor and process until fairly smooth. Heat oil in a skillet and add the tomato purée. Heat 8 to 10 minutes or until thickened. Pour over stuffed zucchini and serve promptly. Great with rice and black beans.

*Martha Kipcak*

## COUNTY FAIR 1982

From the collection of
Bob and Marian Archer, San Antonio, Texas

Every summer the residents of Gillespie County look forward to the close of summer days with the celebration of the County Fair, the oldest continually held county fair in Texas. Whether entering a contest or simply admiring the abundance of local goods, everyone enjoys the Fair.

# Applesauce Raisin Bread

2 1/2 cups flour
1 1/4 cups sugar
1 Tbsp. baking powder
1 tsp. salt
1 1/2 tsp. baking soda
1 tsp. cinnamon
1 cup raisins
1 cup chopped pecans
2 eggs
1 cup applesauce
1/2 cup oil

Place all dry ingredients into a large bowl. Stir in raisins and nuts. Combine the eggs, applesauce, and oil. Add to the dry ingredients and stir just until blended. Divide dough between four mini-loaf pans and bake in preheated 350 degree oven about 50 minutes. Cool on wire racks. Makes 4 mini-loaves.

*Melissa Miller*

# Apricot Bread

2/3 cup dried apricots
1 1/3 cups milk, scalded
2/3 cup Grape Nuts
1 egg, well beaten
3 Tbsp. melted
  shortening
2 cups sifted flour
2/3 cups packed light
  brown sugar
2 1/2 tsp. baking
  powder
1 tsp. salt

Cook apricots half as long as directed on package. Drain, cool, and cut into pieces. Pour milk over cereal, add apricots, cool. Stir in egg and shortening. Mix dry ingredients, add to cereal, stir only enough to dampen flour. Pour into greased 8"x4"x3" pan. Bake 350 degrees for 1 hour or until cake tester comes out clean. Cool in pan 10 minutes, turn out on rack, and cool completely. Slices better the next day. Good with cream cheese spread.

*Jeannine Miller*

# Best Ever Beer Bread

1/2 cup water
1 cup beer
3 Tbsp. oil
3-6 cups all purpose flour
2 packages dry yeast
3 Tbsp. sugar
1 1/2 tsp. salt

Heat the water, beer, and oil to 120 to 130 degrees and set aside.

Combine 2 cups of the flour, yeast, sugar, and salt. Add cooled beer mixture. Beat 5 minutes. Stir in enough remaining flour to make soft dough. Knead until smooth. Place in a greased bowl. Let rise. Punch down and knead. Makes 2 loaves. Bake 375 degrees for 30 to 35 minutes.

*Elsie Specht*

# Bran Buds Bread

1 Tbsp. salt
1/2 tsp. baking soda
2 pkgs. dry yeast
2/3 cup lukewarm water
1 1/2 cups Bran Buds
2 cups buttermilk
4 Tbsp. margarine
6 3/4 to 7 cups sifted flour
3 Tbsp. brown sugar

Dissolve yeast in luke warm water. Heat buttermilk and margarine to lukewarm, add sugar and salt. Add Bran Buds, 3 cups flour, and soda. Mix well. Add yeast and remaining flour. Mix well. Dough should clean the sides of bowl. Knead 10 minutes. Place in greased bowl, turning once. Cover and let rise about 1 1/2 hours. Punch down and divide into 3 loaves. Let rest 15 minutes. Place in 3 well greased loaf pans. Cover and let rise again, about 1 hour and 15 minutes.

Bake at 350 degrees 40 to 45 minutes. Remove from pans and cover with cloth until cool.

*Ruth V. Nettle*

# Currant Scones

| | |
|---|---|
| 2 cups all purpose flour | 6 Tbsp. butter |
| 2 Tbsp. sugar | 1/3 cups dried currants |
| 1 Tbsp. baking powder | 1 beaten egg |
| 1/2 tsp. salt | 1/2 cup milk |
| | 1 slightly beaten egg |

In a mixing bowl stir together flour, sugar, baking powder, and salt. Cut in butter until mixture resembles coarse crumbs. Stir in currants. Add the first beaten egg and milk, stir just until dough clings together. Knead gently on a lightly floured surface (12 to 15 strokes). Cut dough in half. Shape each half into a ball. Pat or roll to a 6" circle. Cut each circle into 8 wedges. Place wedges on an ungreased baking sheet so sides of wedges do not touch. Brush with slightly beaten egg. Bake in a 425 degree oven for 10 minutes. Serve warm with butter and jam. Makes 16.

*Martha Kipcak*

# Dilly Cheese Bread

| | |
|---|---|
| 3 cups Bisquick mix | 1/2 tsp. dried whole dillweed |
| 1 1/2 cups (6 oz.) shredded sharp cheddar cheese | 1 1/4 cups milk |
| 1 Tbsp. sugar | 1 egg, beaten |
| 1/2 tsp. dried mustard | 1 Tbsp. vegetable oil |

Combine first five ingredients in a large mixing bowl, mix well. Add remaining items, stir just until dry ingredients are moistened. Spoon batter into a greased 9"x5"x3" loaf pan. Bake at 350 degrees for 50 minutes or until bread browns.

*Lindsey Straka*

# Focaccia

(Italian Flat Bread)

| | |
|---|---|
| 4 cups flour | 1/2 stick butter or |
| 2 tsp. salt | margarine, melted |
| 1 pkg. dry yeast | (or olive oil) |
| 1 Tbsp. sugar | Rosemary (optional) |
| 2 cups warm water | |

Combine flour and salt. Dissolve yeast in water, sprinkle with sugar and let stand for 15 minutes. Stir yeast mixture into flour. Cover and let rise for 30 minutes in a warm place. Grease hands and press into an 11"x15" greased jellyroll pan. Let rise another 30 minutes in a warm place. Pour melted butter over dough and sprinkle with rosemary (optional). Bake in a preheated 400 degree oven for 20 minutes, then reduce heat to 300 degrees and bake for 10 minutes. This bread is good fresh from the oven or reheated. Freezes well. (Bread is firm when you cut it.)

*Dr. Charles Schmidt*

# Hush Puppies

| | |
|---|---|
| 1 cup corn meal | 1 green onion, minced |
| 1/2 tsp. salt | 1 egg |
| 1/4 cup water | A sprinkle of garlic |
| | powder (optional) |

Mix and form into balls. Drop in skillet of hot oil or shortening. Fry until brown. Serve at once.

*Catherine Joseffy*

# Irish Soda Bread

| | |
|---|---|
| 3 cups wheat flour | 1 tsp. soda |
| 1 cup all purpose flour | 1 tsp. salt |
| 1 1/2 to 2 cups | 3/4 tsp. baking powder |
| buttermilk | |

Mix dry ingredients, add buttermilk and mix well. Form dough into ball after kneading 3 to 4 minutes. Cut a cross in top and down sides. Bake in 350 degree oven for 40 minutes.

*Catherine Joseffy*

# Mother's No Beat Popovers

| | |
|---|---|
| 2 eggs | 1 cup flour |
| 1 cup milk | $1/2$ tsp. salt |

Break eggs into bowl, add milk, flour, and salt. Mix well with spoon (disregard lumps). Fill greased, heavy muffin pan $3/4$ full. Put in cold oven, set at 450 degrees and turn on heat. Bake 30 minutes. Don't peek for 30 minutes.

*Diane Matthews*

# Olive Cheese Bread

| | |
|---|---|
| $2^1/3$ cups biscuit mix | $1/3$ cup pimiento-stuffed |
| $1/2$ cup grated cheddar cheese (about 2 oz.) | olives, coarsely chopped or sliced |
| $1/4$ tsp. dry mustard | 1 Tbsp. butter, melted |
| $1/8$ tsp. onion powder | $3/4$ cup milk |

Combine biscuit mix, cheese, dry mustard, and onion powder in medium bowl. Add olives, butter (or margarine), and milk. Stir just until ingredients are blended. Turn into greased loaf pan. Bake at 375 degrees for 45 minutes. Serve warm or cold with butter or cream cheese.

*Doris Smith*

# Pineapple Pecan Loaf

| | |
|---|---|
| $1/4$ cup shortening | $1/3$ cup frozen orange juice concentrate, slightly thawed and undiluted |
| $3/4$ cup firmly packed brown sugar | |
| 1 egg | 1 8 oz. can crushed pineapple, undrained |
| 2 cups all purpose flour | |
| 1 tsp. baking soda | $1/2$ cup chopped pecans |
| $1/2$ tsp. salt | |

Cream shortening gradually adding sugar, beating well at medium speed of electric mixer. Mix in egg. Combine flour, soda, and salt; add to creamed mixture alternately with orange juice concentrate, beginning and ending with flour mixture. Stir in pineapple and pecans. Pour batter into a greased and floured loaf pan $8^1/2$"x$4^1/2$"x$2^1/2$". Bake at 350 degrees for 50-55 minutes. Cool in pan 10 minutes. Remove and cool on wire rack.

*Charleen Miller*

# Pita Crisps

| | |
|---|---|
| Pita bread, 5 or 6 | Dried oregano flakes |
| 1 stick melted | Parmesan cheese |
| margarine | Parsley flakes |
| Garlic salt | |

Open and separate Pita bread. Using basting brush, brush margarine on inside of each half. Sprinkle each with garlic salt, oregano, parmesan and parsley. (If desired each piece may be quartered.) Bake 12 min. at 350 degrees on cookie sheet.

Store in air tight container when cooled.

You can change the seasonings (Mexican, Creole, etc.).

*Kristine Miller*

# Pull Apart Sticky Buns

| | |
|---|---|
| 1 large pkg. 25 oz. | 1 3 oz. pkg. vanilla or |
| frozen cloverleaf or | butterscotch |
| Parkerhouse rolls | pudding, not |
| (or 2 12 oz. pkgs.) | instant |
| 1 stick butter, melted | 1 tsp. cinnamon |
| | 1/2 cup brown sugar, |
| | packed |
| | 1/2 cup nuts, chopped |

Heavily butter a 10 inch tube pan. Place the frozen rolls in the melted butter and then place in tube pan. Pour remaining butter over the rolls. Combine the remaining ingredients and sprinkle over the rolls. Let stand uncovered on counter overnight. Cover with foil and bake for 20 minutes at 375 degrees or until done. Remove cover and bake 10 minutes to brown. Remove from oven and cool 10 minutes. Invert onto plate. Serves 8.

This is wonderful for breakfast when you have overnight guests plus the aroma from the baking rolls is better than any alarm clock!

*Karen Benignus Laurence*

# Pumpkin Bran Muffins

2 cups bran
$^1/_2$ cup milk
3 eggs
1 16 oz. can pumpkin
$^3/_4$ cup melted
  margarine
$^3/_4$ cup chopped
  pecans

$2^1/_2$ cups flour
2 cups sugar
$1^1/_2$ tsp. cinnamon
1 Tbsp. baking powder
$^1/_2$ tsp. baking soda
2 tsp. grated orange
  rind
$^1/_4$ tsp. ginger

Soak bran, milk, and eggs 5 minutes. Stir in margarine, pumpkin, sugar, flour, baking powder, and soda. Pour in muffin pans or a 9"x12" baking pan. Sprinkle top with nuts. Bake muffins 15-20 minutes at 325 degrees or 35 minutes for cake.

*Sarah Campbell*

# Pumpkin Cheese Bread

$2^1/_2$ cups sugar
1 8 oz. pkg. cream
  cheese softened
$^1/_2$ cup margarine
4 eggs
1 16 oz. can pumpkin

$3^1/_2$ cups flour
2 tsps. baking soda
1 tsp. salt
1 tsp. cinnamon
$^1/_2$ tsp. baking powder
1 cup chopped pecans

Combine sugar, cream cheese, and margarine, mixing at medium speed on electric mixer until well blended. Add eggs, one at a time, mixing well after each addition. Blend in pumpkin. Add combined dry ingredients, mixing just until moistened. Fold in nuts. Pour into 2 greased and floured 9"x5" loaf pans. Bake at 350 degrees, 1 hour or until a wooden pick inserted in center comes out clean. Cool 5 minutes, remove from pans, and cool on wire rack.

*Jeannine Miller*

# Red And Green Chile Pepper Brioche

| | |
|---|---|
| 3 cups all purpose flour | 4 large eggs at room temperature |
| 1¹/₂ Tbsp. sugar | |
| 1 Tbsp. active dry yeast | ¹/₂ cup chopped fresh roasted Anaheim chilie |
| 1¹/₂ tsps. salt | |
| 1 Tbsp. dried hot red pepper flakes | 2³/₄ sticks (1 cup plus 6 Tbsp. unsalted butter, cut into small pieces and softened) |
| ¹/₂ tsp. freshly ground black pepper | |
| 2 Tbsp. milk | |

In mixing bowl combine the flour, sugar, yeast, salt, red pepper, and black pepper. Using an electric mixer, beat in the milk, 1¹/₂ Tbsp. water, eggs (1 at a time) beating well after each addition. Add the chilie. Knead the dough on a floured surface with heavily floured hands until dough is soft and barely holds its shape. The dough will be sticky. Add the butter, 1 piece at a time. Continue to knead the dough until the butter is distributed evenly. Transfer the dough to a buttered bowl. Turn it to coat with butter and let rise, covered with plastic wrap, in a warm place for 3 hours or until double in bulk. Punch the dough down and chill, covered with plastic wrap, for at least 6 hours or overnight. Let the dough rise, covered with plastic wrap, at room temperature for 3-4 hours or until double in bulk. Punch down and transfer into a buttered loaf pan 9"x5"x2¹/₂". Let dough rise for 1 hour, or until double in bulk. Bake in the middle of a preheated 400 degree oven for 30 to 40 minutes, or until golden brown and sounds hollow when tapped. Turn out onto a rack and let it cool.

*Martha Kipcak*

# San Jacinto Inn Biscuits

4 cups flour
3 tsps. baking powder
1 tsp. salt
1 tsp. sugar
3/4 cup shortening
1 3/4 cup milk

Sift flour and dry ingredients in mixing bowl. Add shortening and milk, work with hands on lightly floured board. Roll out and cut with biscuit cutter. Bake in 400 to 425 degree oven until brown (10 to 12 minutes). Yield 20 large biscuits.

*June Miller*

# Sour Cream Biscuits

*Quick And Easy*

2 cups self-rising flour
1 8 oz. carton of sour
   cream
1 stick of margarine

Melt margarine, stir in sour cream, add flour and mix thoroughly. Drop from a mixing spoon into hot buttered muffin tins. Bake at 375 degrees until puffy and lightly browned.

*Doris Smith*

# Sour Cream Coffee Cake

1 stick (4 oz.)
   margarine
1 1/2 cups sugar
2 eggs
2 tsp. vanilla
8 oz. of sour cream
2 cups flour
1 tsp. baking powder
1/2 tsp. baking soda
TOPPING:
2 Tbsp. sugar
2 tsp. cinnamon
1/2 cup pecans, finely
   chopped

With mixer, cream margarine and sugar. Add eggs, vanilla, and sour cream. Sift flour, baking powder, and soda and add to creamed mixture. Combine the 2 Tbsp. sugar, cinnamon and pecans in a small bowl. Pour half the batter into a well greased 10" tube pan, and sprinkle half the cinnamon mixture over the batter. Add remaining batter and sprinkle the rest of the cinnamon mixture over the top. Bake at 350 degrees for 40 minutes.

*Shirley Crooks*

# Southwestern Spoon Bread

| | |
|---|---|
| 1 16¹/₂ oz. can cream style corn | 1 Tbsp. baking powder |
| 1 cup yellow cornmeal | ¹/₂ tsp. salt |
| ³/₄ cup milk | 1 4 oz. can chopped green chilies |
| ¹/₃ cup vegetable oil | 1 cup 4 oz. shredded cheddar cheese |
| 2 eggs, lightly beaten | |

In a mixing bowl stir together all ingredients except last two. Pour half the batter into a greased 2 qt. baking dish. Sprinkle with chilies and cheese. Pour remaining batter over all. Bake at 375 degrees for about 45 minutes or just until set. Serve warm with a spoon. Yield: about 6 to 8 servings.

*Dorothy Russell*

# Whole Wheat Rolls

| | |
|---|---|
| 1 pkg. dry yeast | ¹/₄ cup margarine |
| ¹/₄ cup warm water (110 degrees - 115 degrees) | ¹/₃ cup sugar |
| 1 tsp. sugar | ¹/₂ tsp. salt |
| ³/₄ cup milk, scalded | 3 cups whole wheat flour |
| 1 egg, beaten | |

Soften yeast in warm water. Let sit about ten minutes. Combine milk, shortening, sugar, salt, and cool to lukewarm. Add 1 cup flour, beat well. Add yeast and beaten egg. Mix and add remaining flour. Mix well. Place in greased bowl and let rise to double (grease top of dough). Can be put in refrigerator overnight. Divide in half, roll to about 9" circle ¹/₄" thick. Cut in pie slices and roll as for crescent rolls. Bake at 375 degrees for 12 minutes.

*Delores Sinks*

LEE ETHEL

## CHILDREN'S FOURTH OF JULY PARADE  1985

From the collection of
Peggy Cox, Fredericksburg, Texas

The gazebo and restored library is the location for the annual fourth of July children's parade. A rousing rendition of patriotic songs, inspiring speeches and a grand march of costumed children, dogs, wagons, bicycles make a festive occasion of the day.

# Amazin' Raisin Cake

3 cups unsifted flour
2 cups sugar
1 cup Hellmann's
  mayonnaise
1/3 cup milk
2 eggs
2 tsp. baking soda
1 1/2 tsp. cinnamon
1/2 tsp. nutmeg
1/2 tsp. salt
3 cups apples
1 cup raisins
1/2 cup chopped
  walnuts

Grease and flour 2 (9") round baking pans. In large bowl with mixer at low speed beat first 10 ingredients 2 minutes scraping bowl frequently or beat vigorously 300 strokes by hand. Batter will be very thick. With spoon, stir in peeled, chopped apples, raisins and nuts. Spoon batter into pans. Bake for 45 minutes at 350 degrees or until tester inserted in center comes out clean. Cool in pans 10 min. Remove and cool. Fill and frost with 2 cups whipped cream.

*Jeannine Miller*

# Apple Walnut Cake

1 cup margarine
2 cups sugar
3 eggs
3 cups sifted flour
1 1/2 tsp. baking soda
1/2 tsp. salt
1 tsp. cinnamon
1/4 tsp. mace
2 tsp. vanilla
3 cups chopped apples
2 cups chopped
  walnuts

Cream sugar and margarine together. Add eggs. Sift together next 5 ingredients. Add to mixture. Add last 3 ingredients. Pour batter into greased and floured bundt pan. Bake 90 minutes at 350 degrees. Cool 10 minutes in pan. Invert on cake plate.

*Nancy O'Neal*

# Chocolate Cake With Fudge Frosting

2<sup>1</sup>/<sub>2</sub> squares

2¹/₂ squares
unsweetened
chocolate
1 stick margarine
2 cups sugar
2 eggs

¹/₂ cup buttermilk
1 cup boiling water
2 tsp. vanilla
2 cups flour
¹/₄ tsp. baking soda

Melt chocolate and margarine together in double boiler. In a bowl beat sugar, eggs, buttermilk, boiling water, and vanilla. Add chocolate mixture. Fold in flour and soda. Mix well, but gently. Bake in 2 greased 8" cake pans for 30 minutes at 325 degrees.

FUDGE FROSTING:
1 ¹/₂ squares
unsweetened
chocolate

2 cups sugar
8 oz. whipping cream
2 Tbsp. margarine
1 tsp. vanilla

Melt chocolate in double boiler. With pot over straight heat, add sugar and whipping cream. Cook to 234 degrees. Remove from heat. Add butter and vanilla. Beat until consistency is spreadable (For faster thickening, place pan in a bowl of ice water). Frost cake immediately

*Nancy O'Neal*

# Chocolate Mousse Cake

12 oz. semisweet
  chocolate morsels
3 Tbsp. water
3 Tbsp. powdered
  sugar
7 eggs separated
1 tsp. vanilla

24 ladyfingers
3 Tbsp. light rum
2 cups heavy cream,
  whipped
1/2 square
  unsweetened
  chocolate curls

Melt chocolate with water in double boiler. Add sugar and mix well. Cool slightly. Add egg yolks and mix well. Cool slightly. Add vanilla. Beat egg whites until stiff and fold into mixture. Line sides and bottom of 9"x8"x2³/₄" loaf pan, or spring pan with plastic wrap. Place row of ladyfingers (unsplit) very close together along bottom of pan. Sprinkle with 1/3 of rum and pour on half of chocolate mixture. Repeat. Finish with a third layer of ladyfingers sprinkled with rum. Chill for 24 hours. To serve, turn upside down on chilled platter. Remove plastic wrap carefully. Cover sides and top with whipped cream. Spread top with chocolate curls. Serve in slices. Serves 10.

*Mary Lindsey*

# Chocolate Sheik Cake

2 cups sifted flour
2 cups sugar
1 stick margarine
1/2 cup shortening
4 Tbsp. cocoa
  (heaping)
1 cup water
1/2 cup buttermilk
2 eggs (slightly beaten)
1/2 tsp. soda
1 tsp. cinnamon

1 tsp. vanilla
CAKE ICING:
1 stick margarine
4 Tbsp. cocoa
  (heaping)
6 Tbsp. milk
1 box powdered sugar,
  sifted
1 tsp. vanilla
1 cup pecan halves

In large bowl mix flour and sugar. Bring margarine, shortening, cocoa, and water to a boil in a saucepan. Pour boiling mixture over sugar and flour. Add remaining ingredients. Mix batter well and bake in greased and floured pan 13"x9"x2¹/₂" for 20 minutes at 400 degrees.

To make icing: Melt margarine, add cocoa and milk, bring to a boil and add powdered sugar, vanilla and pecans. Spread over cake and refrigerate.

*Elsie Specht*

# Cream Cheese Pound Cake

| | |
|---|---|
| 3 sticks of butter or margarine | 8 oz. pkg. cream cheese |
| 3 cups sugar | 2 tsp. vanilla |
| 3 cups flour | 1 tsp. lemon extract |
| 6 eggs | 1 tsp. almond extract |

Cream butter and cream cheese. Add sugar. Beat until fluffy. Add flavoring, one of above or all. (I use all of them.) Add flour and eggs, beginning and ending with flour. Pour batter into greased and floured bundt pan. Bake at 325 degrees for one hour or until toothpick inserted comes out clean.

*Sande Knapp*

# Dump Cake

| | |
|---|---|
| 1 pkg. yellow cake mix | 1 can cherry pie filling |
| 1 20 oz. can crushed pineapple, undrained | 1 cup chopped pecans |
| | 1 stick butter, cut in thin slices |

Dump pineapple, then cherry pie filling in greased 9"x13" pan, then dry cake mix. Sprinkle nuts over all. Then place butter slices. Bake 350 degrees for 50 minutes.

*Betty Ethel*

# Rum Cake — Sinful

| | |
|---|---|
| 1 cup chopped pecans | 1/2 cup oil, canola |
| 1 pkg. yellow cake mix | 1/2 cup rum, Bacardi light |
| 1 3 oz. pkg. vanilla instant pudding | |
| 4 eggs | |
| 1/2 cup water | |

Grease bundt pan with margarine. Sprinkle nuts on bottom of pan. Mix yellow cake mix, pudding, water, oil, and rum. Beat eggs in one at a time. Pour into bundt pan and bake 1 hour at 325 degrees. Cool!

SAUCE:
| | |
|---|---|
| 1/4 cup water | 2 oz. (4 Tbsp.) rum |
| 1 stick butter | 1 cup sugar |

For sauce: Boil butter, sugar, water, and rum in a sauce pan. Pour over cake while in pan. Let sauce soak into pan completely before removing. This cake freezes well.

*C. C. Gibbons*

# Four Layer Delight

1 cup flour
1 stick margarine
1 cup chopped pecans
1 8 oz. pkg. cream
    cheese
1 cup powdered sugar
1 qt. whipped topping
2 small pkgs. any
    flavor instant
    pudding
3 cups milk

Mix flour melted margarine and pecans. Press into bottom of 12"x8" pan. Bake at 375 degrees for 15 minutes. Cool.

Mix cream cheese, powdered sugar, and 1 cup whipped topping. Beat thoroughly. Spread over crust.

Mix pudding and milk until thickened. Spread over cheese. Top with remaining whipped topping. Refrigerate. Serves 8 to 10 deliciously.

*Betty Robinson*

# German Sweet Chocolate Cake

1 stick butter
$1/2$ cup crisco
1 cup hot water
1 package German
    Sweet Chocolate
2 cups flour
2 cups sugar
$1/2$ cup buttermilk
2 eggs
1 tsp. baking soda
1 tsp. vanilla
1 tsp. cinnamon

Melt butter, crisco, chocolate, and water in large dutch oven. Remove from heat. Add remaining ingredients. Mix well; batter will be runny. Bake in 13"x9"pan 25 minutes at 350 degrees.

**ICING:**
1 stick butter
6 Tbsp. coffee
1 package German
    Sweet Chocolate
1 box of powdered
    sugar
1 tsp. vanilla
1 cup coconut
1 cup pecans

Melt together butter, coffee and chocolate. Add remaining ingredients. Spread on HOT cake.

*Sande Knapp*

# Gibbon's Patriotic Cake Roll

| | |
|---|---|
| 1 cup flour | 1 pt. blueberries |
| 2 Tbsp. baking powder | 2 pts. strawberries |
| 1/4 tsp. salt | 1 pt. whipping cream |
| 4 eggs | or alternate |
| 1 cup sugar | Powdered sugar |
| 1/4 cup cold water | |

Sift and mix flour, baking powder, and salt. Beat eggs until thick. Add cold water and sugar, beating well. Gradually fold in sifted mixture. Add vanilla. Pour into well greased 10"x15" pan lined with greased waxed paper. Bake 12 to 15 minutes at 450 degrees(pre-heated). DO NOT OVERCOOK. Place waxed paper on table, dust with powdered sugar. Turn hot cake onto waxed paper, roll, wrap with towel and cool in refrigerator.

Slice strawberries in long thin slices. Wash blueberries and set aside. Whip cream. When cake is cool, unroll, spread whipped cream over cake, (I sometimes add a little Grand Marnier to whipped cream and the strawberries) and add sliced strawberries (reserve some for decorating the outside of the cake), plus blueberries. Reroll cake with open portion on the bottom...it will look like a long log. Spread outside of cake with whipped cream. The upper left hand corner is reserved for blueberries to make the star portion of the flag. Then use the long sliced strawberries, end to end to form stripes the length of the cake.

*Helen B. McDonald*

# Gloria's Famous Carrot Cake

3 cups carrots (grated)
1/2-1 cup pecans
2 cups flour (sifted)
2 tsp. soda
2 tsp. cinnamon
1 tsp. salt
4 eggs, separated
2 cups sugar
1 1/2 cups salad oil

Sift together flour, soda, cinnamon, and salt. Separate eggs, beat yolks in a large mixing bowl. Add sugar and salad oil. Add flour mixture to egg yolks, then add carrots and nuts. Beat egg whites and fold into batter. Bake at 325 degrees for 30 minutes in three 10" pans or 45 minutes in a 9"x13" pan.

**ICING:**
1 8 oz. pkg. cream
   cheese softened
3/4 stick butter or
   margarine
1 tsp. vanilla
1 box powdered sugar

Mix well and spread on cooled cake.

*Gloria Hall*

# Kitsi's Cheesecake

1 9" Graham cracker
   crust
3 8 oz. pkgs. cream
   cheese
3/4 cup sugar
3 Tbsp. lemon juice
1 tsp. lemon rind
3 eggs
1 cup sour cream
1/2 Tbsp. vanilla
1/3 cup sugar

Mix together cream cheese, sugar, lemon juice and rind. Add eggs one at a time. Pour in crust and bake for 50-55 minutes at 300 degrees. When done remove, leave oven on. Mix together the sour cream, vanilla, and sugar, and spread on top of cake. Bake 10 minutes more at 300 degrees. Top with strawberries.

*Patti Richard*

# Little Phyllo Cheesecakes

**8 sheets frozen phyllo pastry, thawed**
**1¹/₂ tsp. grated orange rind**
**1 Tbsp. orange juice**
**¹/₂ cup orange marmalade**
**2 tsp. orange juice**

**3 oz. pkgs. cream cheese, softened**
**¹/₂ cup butter or margarine, melted**
**¹/₂ cup sifted powdered sugar**

Place 1 sheet of phyllo on a damp towel (keep remaining phyllo covered). Lightly brush phyllo on first sheet, brushing each with butter. Cut each stack of phyllo into 3-inch squares, using kitchen shears. Brush miniature muffin cups with melted butter. Place one square of layered phyllo into each muffin cup, pressing gently in center to form a pastry shell.

Combine cream cheese, powdered sugar, orange rind, and 1 Tbsp. orange juice; beat at high speed with electric mixer until blended and smooth. Spoon 1¹/₂ tsp. mixture into each pastry shell.

Bake at 350 degrees for 8 to 10 minutes or until golden. Gently remove from pan, and let cool on wire rack. Make another stack of 4 buttered sheets of phyllo. Cut each stack of phyllo into 3-inch squares.

Combine orange marmalade and 2 tsp. orange juice; top each cheesecake with ¹/₂ tsp. orange marmalade mixture. Yield 40 pastries.

NOTE: Phyllo shells may be made up to 2 days in advance; store in an airtight container. Fill shells up to 4 hours before serving. Chill until ready to serve.

*Alethia Alt & Doris Smith*

# Mama Lena's Ginger Cake

1 cup molasses
3/4 cup water
1/2 cup shortening
2 3/4 cups flour
1 tsp. (each): salt,
    cinnamon, ginger
2 tsp. baking powder
1/2 tsp. baking soda in
3 Tbsp. hot water

1 egg
SAUCE:
3/4 cup sugar
1 cup water
1 Tbsp. cornstarch
2 Tbsp. lemon juice or
    1 small can crushed
    pineapple

Mix in a sauce pan molasses, water, and shortening and bring to a boil. Sift flour, salt, cinnamon, ginger, baking powder and add to boiled mixture. Add one egg. Pour into greased and floured 13"x9" pan. Bake at 350 degrees until knife inserted comes out clean. About 30 minutes.

SAUCE FOR GINGER CAKE: Cook in saucepan just until thick; sugar, water, cornstarch, lemon juice or pineapple. Pour over squares of cake.

*Micki George*

# Mary Ann's Cupcakes

1 cup butter
2 cups sugar
4 eggs, separated
3 cups flour, sifted
1 tsp. salt

1 cup milk
1 tsp. vanilla
3 tsp. baking powder
1 cup pecans, chopped
1 cup raisins

Beat the butter and sugar until very light and creamy. Add the well-beaten egg yolks. Add flour with salt and baking powder. Add milk a little at a time with flour. Add vanilla, raisins and pecans. Fold in beaten egg whites. Put batter in muffin tins. Bake at 375 degrees 25 minutes. May be topped with icing.

*Mary Ann Taylor*

# Prune Cake

1 cup cut, pitted prunes
1 cup boiling water
2 cups flour
1 1/2 cups sugar
1 tsp. each of salt, cinnamon, nutmeg, cloves
1 1/4 tsp. baking soda
1/2 cup oil
3 eggs, slightly beaten
1 cup chopped nuts
2 cups powdered sugar, sifted
1 ounce or so of rum

Pour boiling water over prunes and let stand 2 hours. Mix flour, sugar, salt, spices, and soda; add to prunes. Stir in oil, eggs, and nuts. Pour into a greased and floured 9"x13" pan. Bake at 350 degrees until firm in middle (about 35 minutes). Time depends on pan. To make icing: mix powdered sugar and rum enough to make a thick, but spreadable paste. Poke holes with a fork into warm cake and spread on the icing or slice cake sideways and use as a filling.

*Micki George*

# Punch Bowl Cake

1 box yellow cake mix, prepared by package directions
2 cans cherry pie filling
2 3 oz. instant vanilla pudding, prepared
2 8 1/4 ounce cans crushed pineapple
4 bananas
2 8 oz. cartons frozen whipped topping, thawed
1 cup chopped pecans
1 cup shredded coconut

Use a large punch bowl or large clear bowl. Crumble half of cake onto bottom. Top with a layer of cherry pie filling, then layers of pudding, pineapple, sliced bananas, whipped topping, pecans and coconut. Repeat layers. Save a few cherries, pecans and pineapple bits for a garnish. Chill.

*A favorite for large crowds.*

*David Smith*

# Pumpkin Cheesecake

**CRUST:**
³/₄ cup graham cracker crumbs
¹/₂ cup finely chopped pecans
¹/₄ cup firmly packed dark brown sugar
¹/₄ cup granulated sugar
¹/₂ stick (¹/₄ cup) unsalted butter, melted and cooled

**FILLING:**
1 cup canned pumpkin purée

3 large eggs at room temperature
1¹/₂ tsp. ground cinnamon
¹/₂ tsp. freshly grated nutmeg
¹/₂ tsp. ground ginger
¹/₂ tsp. salt
1 cup plus 2 tablespoons granulated sugar
1¹/₂ lbs. cream cheese, softened
2 Tbsp. heavy cream
1 Tbsp. cornstarch
1 tsp. vanilla

To make crust: combine the crumbs, pecans, sugars, and butter. Press mixture onto the bottom of a 10-inch springform pan, and freeze the crust for 15 minutes.

To make filling: In a bowl whisk together well the pumpkin, eggs, cinnamon, nutmeg, ginger, salt, and ³/₄ cup of granulated sugar. In another bowl with an electric mixer cream together the cream cheese and remaining 6 Tbsp. granulated sugar, beat in the cream, cornstarch, and the vanilla, and beat in the pumpkin mixture. Pour the filling into the crust in the pan and bake the cheesecake in the middle of a preheated 350 degree oven for 40 to 45 minutes, or until the center is set. Cool cheesecake in the pan on a rack and chill it, covered loosely, overnight. Run a knife around the inside edge of pan and remove the side of the pan.

Optional garnish: whipped cream, cinnamon sugar, crushed toffee candy.

*THE PEACH TREE TEA ROOM, Fredericksburg*

# Shortcut Cointreau Cake

| 1 box yellow cake mix | 1 carton whipped |
| 1 pkg. vanilla pudding | topping, thawed |
| mix | $^1/_4$ cup plus 1 Tbsp. |
| Grated rind of 2 | Cointreau liquor |
| oranges (eat the | |
| oranges) | |

Prepare cake mix and pudding as directed on boxes. Add grated rind to pudding while still hot. Allow to cool. Split each cake layer, sprinkle cut surfaces with liquor. Place $^1/_2$ layer on plate. Cover with $^1/_3$ of pudding, add other layers with pudding, ending with a smooth surface on top. Frost with whipped topping. Decorate with mandarin orange segments if desired. Store in refrigerator.

*Barbara Ann Pressler*

# Red, White And Blue Cheesecakes

| 2 8 oz. pkgs. cream | 1 tsp. vanilla |
| cheese | 1 can cherry pie filling |
| $^3/_4$ cup sugar | 1 can blueberry pie |
| 2 eggs, beaten | filling |
| 1 tsp. vanilla | 1 pkg. of 2 inch foil |
| 1 box vanilla wafers | cupcakes holders |
| 1 pint sour cream | (for baking) |
| $^1/_3$ cup sugar | |

Be sure all paper linings are removed from foil cups. Add vanilla wafer to bottom of each cupcake holder. Combine cream cheese and sugar; add eggs, vanilla and beat until smooth. Fill cups $^3/_4$ full. Bake at 375 degrees for 12 minutes. Remove, leaving oven on. Mix sour cream, sugar, and vanilla. Spread on top of hot cheesecakes, and return to oven for two minutes. When cool put 1 tsp. of either pie filling on each cake.

*Doris Smith*

# All Time Favorite Cereal Cookies

| | |
|---|---|
| 1/2 cup. margarine | 1/4 tsp. baking soda |
| 1/2 cup sugar | 1/2 tsp. baking powder |
| 1/2 cup brown sugar | 1 cup rolled oats |
| 1/2 tsp. vanilla | 1 cup cornflakes or |
| 1 egg | your favorite cereal |
| 1 cup flour | 1/2 cup coconut |
| 1/8 tsp. salt | |

Cream together margarine, sugars and vanilla. Add egg and vanilla. Mix until smooth. Sift flour, baking soda, baking powder, and salt together. Add to sugar mixture. Blend in oats, cereal and coconut. Drop from teaspoon onto cookie sheet. Bake at 325 degrees for 15 minutes.

*Velna Jackson*

# Billy Goats

| | |
|---|---|
| 1 cup margarine | 1 tsp. ground |
| 1 1/2 cup sugar | cinnamon |
| 3 egg yolks | 1/4 tsp. ground cloves |
| 1 tsp. vanilla | 2 Tbsp. sour milk |
| 2 1/2 cups flour | 4 cups chopped |
| 1 tsp. soda | walnuts |
| 1/8 tsp. salt | 1 pound chopped dates |

Cream margarine and sugar well; add egg yolks and vanilla and beat with electric mixer at medium speed for 2-3 minutes or by hand until light and fluffy. Sift together flour, soda, salt, and spices. Add dry ingredients to egg mixture with sour milk. Blend well by hand. Add walnuts and dates and work in well. Drop by the teaspoonful 1 inch apart on greased cookie sheet. Bake at 325 degrees 20 minutes.

*June Miller*

# Chocolate Chip Pizza

| | |
|---|---|
| 1/2 cup sugar | 1/2 cup brown sugar |
| 1/2 cup softened butter | 1/2 cup peanut butter |
| 1/2 tsp. vanilla | 1 egg |
| 1 1/2 cups flour | 2 cups miniature marshmallows |
| 6 oz. pkg. chocolate chips | 1 1/2 cups pecans (optional) |

Preheat oven to 375 degrees. In big bowl combine and blend well first six ingredients. Add flour and stir until soft dough forms. Press dough evenly into 12" to 14" pizza pan. Bake 10 minutes at 375 degrees. Remove from oven; sprinkle on remaining ingredients. Bake again for 5 minutes or until marshmallows turn brown and puffy. Cool. Cut into wedges. May store in tightly closed container.

*Mary Ann Smith*

# Eagle Brand Magic Cookie Bars

| | |
|---|---|
| 1/2 cup butter or margarine | 6 ozs. semi-sweet chocolate chips |
| 1 1/2 cups graham cracker crumbs | 3 1/2 oz. flaked coconut |
| 1 cup Eagle Brand Condensed Milk | 1 cup chopped nuts |

Melt butter in a 13"x9" baking pan. Remove from heat; sprinkle crumbs over butter. Pour sweetened condensed milk evenly over crumbs. Top with chocolate chips, coconut, and nuts. Press down gently. Bake at 350 degrees for 25 minutes or until golden brown. Cool. Cut into small squares.

*Bessie Evers*

# Chocolate Iced Cookies

**COOKIE DOUGH:**
1 cup powdered sugar
1 cup soft butter
$1/2$ tsp. salt
2 cup flour
**FILLING:**
1 cup powdered sugar
2 Tbsp. flour
1 tsp. vanilla
3 oz. soft cream
    cheese

$1/2$ cup chopped
    pecans
$1/2$ cup coconut
**ICING:**
$1/2$ cup chocolate
    chips
$1/2$ cup powdered sugar
2 Tbsp. butter
2 Tbsp. water

Dough: Cream sugar, butter and salt. Add flour. Shape into balls using 1 tsp. of dough for each. Place 2 inches apart on cookie sheet. Make thumb print in each ball. Bake at 350 degrees for 12-15 minutes or until golden.

Filling: Mix sugar, flour, vanilla, cheese, coconut, and water together and have ready. Fill each cookie with $1/2$ tsp. filling as soon as cookies come out of the oven.

Icing: In a small saucepan, melt chocolate chips with water and butter. Stir constantly. Remove from heat. Add powdered sugar. Blend until smooth. Drizzle frosting over filling of each cookie. Keep frosting warm while drizzling. Yield: $2^1/2$ dozen cookies.

*Velna Jackson*

# Frosted Chewies

1 cup sugar
1 cup white Karo
1 cup crunchy peanut
  butter
6 cups Special K
  cereal

6 oz. pkg. or 1 cup
  chocolate chips
6 oz. pkg. or 1 cup
  butterscotch chips

Cook sugar and Karo in medium sized sauce pan over medium heat, stirring frequently, until mixture boils. Remove from heat. Add peanut butter, mix well. Then add cereal. Stir until evenly coated. Press mixture firmly into buttered 13"x9" pan (works best with buttered fingers). Melt chocolate and butterscotch chips together in top of double boiler or microwave oven. Spread evenly over cereal mixture. Cut into 2"x1" bars when cool. Makes 4 dozen.

*Jeannine Miller*

# Grandmother's Tea Cakes

1 cup butter
2 cups sugar
2 eggs, slightly beaten
1 cup thick sour
  cream
5 cups pre-sifted flour

2 tsp. baking powder
¹/₂ teaspoon baking
  soda
1 tsp. vanilla

Cream butter and sugar thoroughly. Add slightly beaten eggs and vanilla. Add soda dissolved in sour cream, then flour, and baking powder. Blend all together. This dough can be rolled and cut or rolled in wax paper and refrigerated for 24 hours and then sliced. Bake on greased cookie sheet at 425 degrees for 8-10 minutes.

*Mary Ann Taylor*

# Lemon Delight Bars

1 cup butter (or $1/2$ butter and $1/2$ margarine)
$1/2$ cup powdered sugar
2 cups sifted flour
$1/2$ cup nuts, chopped fine
4 eggs, slightly beaten

2 cups sugar
$1/4$ cup sifted flour
Juice of 2 lemons
4 Tbsp. lemon peel, optional
$1/2$ tsp. lemon extract, optional

Mix butter, powdered sugar, flour, and nuts (mix by hand, not with mixer); press into 9"x13" pan. Spread thin and bake 20 minutes at 325 degrees. Stir together eggs, sugar, $1/4$ cup flour, and lemon juice. Pour over first mixture. Bake 20 minutes more at 325 degrees. Remove from oven and sprinkle with powdered sugar. Let cool and cut. YUMMY!

*Jeannine Miller*
*Ruby Edwards*
*Mary Stuart Lundy*

# Macaroons

2 egg whites
1 cup sugar
1 tsp. vanilla

1 cup shredded coconut
2 cups corn flakes
$1/2$ cup chopped nuts

Heat oven to 400 degrees. Beat egg whites stiff. Add sugar slowly, continuing to beat. Fold in rest of ingredients. Drop by rounded teaspoonsful, $1/2$" apart on greased cookie sheets. Bake 15 minutes or until lightly browned. Makes 3 dozen.

*Mildred Roper*

## Mrs. O'Field's Cookies

1 cup butter or margarine
1 cup white sugar
1 cup brown sugar
1 tsp. vanilla
2 eggs, beaten
2 cups flour
2½ cups oats, finely ground in blender or processor
½ tsp. salt
1 tsp. baking soda
1 tsp. baking powder
12 oz. chocolate chips (semi-sweet or milk)
4 oz. hershey bar, chocolate grated
1 cup chopped nuts

Preheat oven to 375 degrees. Cream butter and sugars until fluffy, mix in vanilla and beaten eggs. Sift flour, oats, salt, baking powder, and baking soda together and add in batches to the butter mixture. Blend thoroughly. Fold in chocolate chips, grated chocolate bar and nuts. Bake on an ungreased cookie sheet, 2" apart for 8-10 minutes. Makes approximately 7 dozen cookies.

*Nancy O'Neal*

## Oatmeal Raisin Cookies

¼ cup margarine
½ cup brown sugar
½ tsp. cinnamon
¼ cup dry milk solids
½ tsp. baking soda
¼ tsp. baking powder
¼ tsp. salt
¼ tsp. ground cloves
¼ cup chopped nuts
¾ cup whole wheat flour
¾ cup applesauce
½ cup rolled oats
⅓ cup oat bran
½ cup raisins

Combine margarine and sugar well. Mix dry ingredients. Add raisins and nuts. Drop by tablespoon onto cookie sheets. Bake at 375 degrees for about 10 minutes. Cool on rack.

*Micki George*

# Orissa's Sand Tarts

1/2 lb. butter or
  margarine
3 heaping tsp. sugar

3 cups flour
Jam, any flavor
Whole pecan halves

Mix butter, sugar and flour until completely blended. Mold into walnut size balls. Make dent; put a dab of jam in dent; cover with pecan halves. Bake at 275 degrees about 45 minutes or until brown. Roll in powdered sugar while hot.

*C.C. Gibbons*

# Praline Cookies

24 whole graham
  crackers
2 sticks margarine

1 cup brown sugar
1 tsp. light Karo syrup
1 cup chopped pecans

Put graham crackers on large greased cookie sheet. Boil margarine, brown sugar (firmly packed), and syrup for 2 minutes. Remove from heat and add pecans. Mix, then pour and spread over graham crackers. Bake 8 to 10 minutes at 350 degrees. Cool and cut into squares.

*Jeannine Miller*

# Quick Peanut Butter Cookies

1 cup extra crunchy
  peanut butter
1 cup sugar
1 egg

Dash of salt
1 tsp. vanilla
Note: NO FLOUR!

Mix the above ingredients until well blended. You will be able to handle when well mixed.

For each cookie, take small amount of dough; roll into ball; place on ungreased cookie sheet. Press lightly with fork. Bake at 350 degrees for 13 minutes. Makes 4 dozen cookies.

*Kathleen Bridges*

# Ranger Cookies

| | |
|---|---|
| 1 cup shortening | 2 cups flour |
| 1 cup sugar | 2 tsp. baking soda |
| 1 cup brown sugar | 1 tsp. baking powder |
| 2 eggs | 1/2 tsp. salt |
| 2 cups corn flakes, crushed | 1 cup coconut |
| | 1 tsp. vanilla |

Mix well, drop on cookie sheet by spoonful. Bake in 300 degree oven for 12-15 minutes.

*Can use chocolate chips in place of coconut or pecans.

*Elsie Specht*

# Rosettes

| | |
|---|---|
| 2 eggs | 1 cup milk |
| 1 tsp. sugar | 1/4 tsp. salt |
| 1 cup flour | Rosetten iron mold |

Above amount will make about forty patties.

Beat the eggs slightly, add sugar, salt, and milk. Stir in flour gradually, and beat until smooth. Screw handle into mold. Dip iron into hot lard or oil, then into batter, not allowing batter to come over top of the iron. Fry for at least 20 seconds but not more than 35 seconds. Remove from iron with a clean piece of cheesecloth, and allow to cool before serving.

Should the batter fail to adhere to the mold, the iron is probably overheated. If the patties blister undoubtedly the eggs are beaten too much. To insure crisp patties they should be fried somewhat moderately. Patties sufficiently fried will come from the irons freely.

*Jean Wieser*

# Schneckerdudel (Sugar Cookies)

1 cup Crisco
1 cup sugar
2 eggs
$^1/_4$ cup cream
1 tsp. almond
    flavoring
2$^1/_4$ cups flour
2 tsps. cream of tartar
$^1/_2$ tsp. baking soda
Sugar and cinnamon
    mix

Sift flour and cream of tartar. Add other ingredients. Chill dough. Roll dough into balls and turn in sugar and cinnamon. Place 2 inches apart on a greased and floured baking sheet. Bake until lightly browned, but still soft, about 8 to 10 minutes in a 350 degree oven.

*Bessie Evers*

# Turtle Brownies

1 pkg. German
    Chocolate Cake Mix
$^3/_4$ cup margarine
$^1/_3$ cup evaporated
    milk
3 cups chopped nuts
1 pkg. caramels
$^1/_2$ cup evaporated
    milk
1 large 12 oz. pkg.
    chocolate chips

Mix cake mix, margarine and $^1/_3$ cup evaporated milk, plus 2 cups of nuts together. PRESS ONE-HALF OF MIXTURE in a greased and floured 9"x13" pan. Bake at 350 degrees for 8 minutes and take out. Melt caramels with $^1/_2$ cup evaporated milk in a sauce pan over low heat. Leave mixture on stove. Sprinkle chocolate chips and all of the nuts over baked crust and drizzle melted caramels over. Put remaining batter on top. Work with fingers. Will go together when baked. Bake 20 minutes at 350 degrees.

*Doris Schmid*

# Frozen Fruit Dessert

| | |
|---|---|
| 1 8 oz. pkg. cream cheese (room temperature) | 1/2 cup pecans |
| 3/4 cup sugar | 3 bananas, sliced thin |
| 1 large can crushed pineapple (well drained) | 1 10 oz. pkg. frozen strawberries (thawed) |
| | 1 8 oz. carton cool whip |

Mix in large bowl cream cheese and sugar. Add pine-apple, pecans, bananas, and strawberries. Freeze in either loaf pan or 9"x13".

*Good with brown sugar, flour & margarine crust also.*

*Pat Reese*

# Lemon Orange Sherbet

| | |
|---|---|
| 2 1/2 cups sugar | 1 qt. milk |
| 6 lemons juice only (app. 1 cup) | 1 qt. half and half |
| 6 oranges juice only (app. 2 1/2 cups) | 4 egg whites |

Mix and chill juices and sugar; add milk and cream. Fold in stiffly beaten egg whites. Freeze in one gal-lon ice cream freezer. Makes 3 quarts.

*Betty Ethel*

# Milky Way Ice Cream

12 1³/₄ oz. Milky Way
   bars
1 14 oz. sweetened
   condensed milk

1 5.5 oz. chocolate
   syrup
3 qts. milk

Combine condensed milk and cut up Milky Way bars and melt over low heat. Stir until Milky Way bars are completely melted. Let cool. Stir occasionally. Stir in 1 quart of milk and beat until blended. Pour this into your ice cream freezer and stir in can of chocolate syrup. Add the rest of the milk. Mix and freeze. I make this in ice cream freezer then put into freezer containers and store in freezer. Makes 1 gallon.

*Doris Smith*

# Oreo Ice Cream Cake

1 pkg. Oreo Cookies
   (double cookies)
¹/₂ gallon softened
   vanilla ice cream

1 small carton of Cool
   Whip
Chocolate syrup
Chopped nuts

Crumble two rows of Oreo Cookies and place in 13"x9"x2" Pyrex dish. Cover with ice cream. Crumble one row of Oreo Cookies and place over ice cream. Cover with chocolate syrup. Cover syrup with Cool Whip. Sprinkle with chopped nuts. Cover and store in freezer. Cut in squares to serve.

*Gloria Glass*

# American Strudel

| | |
|---|---|
| 1/2 lb. margarine (room temp.) | 1 cup apricot jam |
| 1 cup sour cream | 1 cup golden raisins |
| 2 cups flour | 1 cup chopped nuts |
| | Powdered sugar |

Blend margarine, sour cream and flour. Separate into 4 equal balls. Wrap and chill at least 1 hour. Roll out thin on floured board into a long, narrow (6" wide) strip.

Mix together jam, raisins and nuts. Spread on dough. Roll like a jelly roll. Pinch edges to seal. Place on ungreased baking sheet. Bake 40 minutes at 350 degrees. Remove from oven and dust with powdered sugar.

*Jan Peterson*

# Apple-Almond Upside Down Pie

| | |
|---|---|
| 2 Tbsp. soft butter (or margarine) | 4-5 cups peeled, thinly sliced apples |
| 2/3 cup sliced toasted almonds | 2 Tbsp. cornstarch |
| 1/3 cup light brown sugar | 1/2 tsp. nutmeg |
| | 3/4 cup sugar |
| 2 uncooked pie crusts for 9" pie | 1/4 cup brown sugar |

Preheat oven to 450 degrees. Line 9" pie pan with foil, letting foil hang over edge. Spread with butter. Press almonds into butter and sprinkle with brown sugar. Cover with pastry to make bottom crust.

Mix apples, cornstarch, spices and sugars and let stand 5 minutes. Fill crust with apple mixture. Cover with top pastry and seal edges. Flute edges and prick pastry. Bake 10 minutes. Reduce heat to 375 degrees and bake 35 to 40 minutes. Cool no more than 15 minutes or nuts will stick to foil. Invert onto platter and remove foil.

*Linda Zehnder*

# Apple Strudel

1/2 lb. 1 cup butter or margarine
1/2 pint 1 cup sour cream
2 cups all-purpose flour
1/2 tsp. salt
Chopped nuts

Melted butter
1 cup crushed vanilla wafers
12-16 medium baking apples
1 cup sugar
1 tsp. cinnamon
Raisins, optional

Butter, sour cream and flour should be at room temperature. Put flour, salt and butter in a large bowl. Blend with a pastry cutter until mixture resembles fine cornmeal. Stir in sour cream with fork. Knead until smooth. Divide dough into 2 portions. Wrap each in Saran Wrap and chill overnight. Next day, peel, core and slice 6 to 8 of the apples, not too thinly. Mix sugar and cinnamon. Roll one portion of dough at a time to a not-too-thin 12"x16" rectangle. Brush dough with some melted butter. Sprinkle with 1/2 cup cookie crumbs. Place apple slices down the lengthwise center. Sprinkle them with 1/2 cup of the cinnamon sugar, then scatter pecans and raisins. Fold ends over the apple filling. Then fold the farthest end over as tight as you can without tearing dough. Repeat with nearest end. Transfer strudel to a greased cookie sheet. Repeat with second portion of dough. Both strudels should fit on the sheet. Brush them with melted butter. Bake 1 hour at 375 degrees. NOTE: The dough can be placed on the cookie sheet before filling is added.

*Barbara Ann Pressler*

# Berry Good Cobbler

| | |
|---|---|
| 4 cups berries, picked and washed | 1 cup milk |
| 2 cups sugar | Pinch salt |
| 1 cup flour | Ice cream or heavy cream |
| 2 tsp. baking powder | 3/4 stick margarine |

Bring berries and sugar to a boil and set aside after about 5 minutes of cooking. Sift together flour, sugar, baking powder, salt and work in 1 cup sweet milk. Melt 1/2 to 3/4 stick margarine in an oblong baking dish. Spread dough over margarine. Pour the berries over the dough. Bake at 350 degrees until the dough rises to the top and forms a crust (about 30 minutes). Let the crust brown. Serve warm with heavy cream or ice cream.

*Nancy O'Neal*

# Blackberries & Dumplings

| | |
|---|---|
| 1 qt. blackberries, fresh or frozen | 1 1/4 tsp. baking powder |
| 1 cup sugar | 1 cup sifted regular all-purpose flour |
| 1 tsp. salt | 2 Tbsp. shortening |
| | 1/2 cup milk |

In large saucepan over medium heat, heat blackberries, sugar and 1/4 cup water to boiling. In medium bowl sift flour, baking powder, salt and 2 tablespoons sugar. Cut in shortening. Lightly mix in milk to form soft dough. Drop dough by tablespoons into boiling fruit. Simmer uncovered 10 minutes.

*Rachel Shiflet*

# Brownie Pie

3 egg whites
Pinch of salt
3/4 cup of sugar
3/4 cup finely crushed
  chocolate cookie
  (wafers) crumbs
1 tsp. vanilla
1/2 cup chopped
  pecans or walnuts
1 cup whipped topping
  (or whipped cream)

Beat egg whites and salt until they stand in soft peaks. Add sugar gradually, beating until stiff peaks form. Fold in cookie crumbs, vanilla and nuts. Spoon evenly into lightly buttered 9" pie pan. Bake at 325 degrees about 35 minutes. Cool completely. Spread top with the topping. Chill 3-4 hours.

*Betsy Slyker*

# Butter Nut Brownie Pie

2 egg whites (beaten
  stiff)
1 cup sugar
1 cup graham cracker
  crumbs
1 cup chopped pecans
1/2 pint whipped cream
  or Cool Whip

Blend all ingredients into the egg whites. Place in pie pan. Bake at 350 degrees for 15 minutes or until brown. Top with whipped cream or Cool Whip.

*Gloria Glass*

# Chocolate Pecan Pie

| | |
|---|---|
| 1 1/2 cup pecan halves | 1 cup light corn syrup |
| 3 1 oz. squares | 1/2 cup sugar |
| semisweet | 1 tsp. vanilla extract |
| chocolate | 1/4 tsp. salt |
| 1/4 cup butter or | 3 eggs, lightly beaten |
| margarine | 1 unbaked 9" pie shell |

Place pecans in prepared pastry shell; set aside. Combine chocolate and butter in a medium sauce-pan; cook over low heat until chocolate melts, stirring smooth. Remove from heat and add corn syrup and remaining ingredients, mixing well. Pour mixture over pecans. Bake at 350 degrees for 1 hour or until knife inserted 1 inch from edge comes out clean.

*Sande Knapp*

# Easy Peach Cobbler

| | |
|---|---|
| 3 or 4 cups sliced | 1 cup flour |
| peaches | 1 cup milk |
| 2 cups sugar | 1/4 tsp. salt |
| 1 lemon (juice only) | 2 tsps. baking powder |
| 1 stick margarine | Cinnamon |

To peaches add 1 cup sugar and juice of lemon. Melt margarine in 9"x13" pan. Beat together flour, 1 cup sugar, milk, salt and baking powder. Pour batter on melted margarine (do not mix). Add peaches. Sprinkle with cinnamon. Bake 350 degrees for 1 hour.

*Ruby Edwards*
*Velna Jackson*

# Fresh Strawberry Pie

1 cup sugar
3 Tbsp. cornstarch
3 Tbsp. strawberry
   jello
1 cup water

1 or 2 pints
   strawberries
1 baked pie shell
$^1/_2$ pt. whipping cream
   or whipped topping

Mix and cook sugar, cornstarch, jello and water, stirring, bring to a boil and remove from heat immediately. Cool. Cut berries in half and add. Pour into cooled pie shell. Cover with sweetened whipped cream.

*Sarah Campbell*

# Grasshopper Pie

3 cups mini
   marshmallows or
   32 large
   marshmallows
$^1/_2$ cup milk
$^1/_4$ cup creme de
   menthe

3 Tbsp. white creme
   de cocoa
$1^1/_2$ cup whipped
   cream
CRUST:
$1^1/_2$ cup oreo crumbs
2 tsps. flour
$^1/_4$ cup margarine

Make crust by stirring together crumbs, flour and margarine and pressing $1^1/_4$ cups into a 9" pie pan, reserving $^1/_4$ cup crumbs for topping.

Make filling by melting marshmallows over medium heat with milk. Then refrigerate until thick. Stir in the creme de menthe and creme de cocoa. Fold in the whipped cream. Pour into crust; sprinkle remaining crumbs on top. Refrigerate until serving time.

*Sarah Campbell*

# Peach Crisp Cobbler

| | |
|---|---|
| 6 cups sliced fresh peaches | $^1/_2$ tsp. salt |
| $1/_4$ cup butter, softened | $^1/_4$ tsp. ground nutmeg |
| $1^3/_4$ cups of sugar | 1 Tbsp. cornstarch |
| divided | (more for frozen peaches) |
| 1 tsp. baking powder | 1 cup boiling water |
| 1 cup all-purpose flour | Whipping cream or ice |
| $^1/_2$ cup of milk | cream, optional |

Place peach slices in large (deep) oblong baking pan. Cream butter and $^3/_4$ cup sugar. Combine flour, baking powder and salt; add to creamed mixture alternately with milk. Spoon mixture over fruit. Leave space between drops of mixture. Sift together 1 cup sugar, cornstarch and nutmeg; sprinkle over batter. Pour boiling water over top. Bake at 350 degrees 1 hour. Serve with whipping cream or ice cream, if desired. Yield 18 servings. Note: Omit boiling water when using frozen peaches as these are much juicer.

*Mrs. Jerry Parsons*

# Lemon Chess Pie

| | |
|---|---|
| $1^1/_2$ cups sugar | $^1/_4$ tsp. salt |
| 1 Tbsp. cornmeal | $^1/_3$ cup softened butter |
| 1 Tbsp. flour | 1 Tbsp. grated lemon peel |
| $^1/_3$ cup lemon juice | 1 tsp. vanilla |
| 4 large eggs | 1 unbaked 9" pie shell |
| $^1/_2$ cup buttermilk | |

Combine sugar, corn meal, and flour with $^1/_4$ tsp. salt. Beat eggs well; add sugar mixture. Add butter-milk, butter, lemon peel, lemon juice and vanilla. Beat well. Pour into pie shell. Bake at 350 degrees about 40 minutes or until top is golden brown. (There will be some free standing butter at this stage, but it is absorbed as pie cools.)

*Jim Muncey*

# Peasant Pecan Pie

5 egg whites
1 1/2 cup sugar
1 tsp. baking powder
1 tsp. vanilla

20 Ritz crackers
2 cup chopped pecans
10" glass pie plate

Beat egg whites until stiff, but not dry. Mix together sugar, baking powder and vanilla. Blend slowly into egg whites. Crush Ritz crackers, but not too fine; toss with pecans. Use spatula to gently fold together egg white mixture, pecans and crackers. Mix only enough to mix dry and wet ingredients evenly. Pour into greased pie plate and bake in pre-heated 350 degree oven for 25 to 30 minutes, or until golden brown, top and bottom. Chill and top with whipped cream.

*Pat Reese*

# Pecan Pie

1 cup sugar
1 cup Karo syrup
1 cup whole pecan
   halves
3 eggs

1 tsp. vanilla
1 unbaked pie shell,
   9 1/2"
1 or 2 tsp. butter
Pinch of salt

Combine sugar, syrup and eggs. DO NOT PRICK BOTTOM OF SHELL. Cover bottom of pie shell with whole pecan halves and dot with butter. Pour sugar mixture into pie shell. Sprinkle lightly with salt. Bake at 400 degrees for 5 minutes. Reduce heat to 300 degrees. Bake for 1 hour.

*Nell Simes*
*C. C. Gibbons*
*Gloria Jones*

# Pineapple Meringue Pie

| | |
|---|---|
| 1 baked pie shell | ¹/₈ tsp. salt |
| 1 20 oz. can crushed | 3 egg yolks |
| pineapple | 1 Tbsp. lemon juice |
| ³/₄ cup sugar | |
| 2 Tbsp. flour | |

Drain pineapple; reserve ¹/₂ cup syrup. Combine sugar, flour and salt in medium saucepan. Stir in pineapple, reserved syrup, sour cream, egg yolks and lemon juice. Cook over medium heat, stirring constantly, until mixture boils and is thick. Cover. Cool to lukewarm. Pour into baked pie shell. Top with meringue. Bake at 350 degrees 12 to 15 minutes until golden brown.

**NEVER EVER FAIL MERINGUE:**

| | |
|---|---|
| 2 Tbsp. sugar | ¹/₈ tsp. salt |
| 1 Tbsp. cornstarch | ¹/₂ tsp. vanilla |
| ¹/₂ cup water | 6 Tbsp. sugar |
| 3 egg whites | |

Combine 2 Tbsp. sugar and cornstarch in small saucepan. Add water. Cook over medium heat, stirring constantly, until mixture is thick and clear. Cool. Beat egg whites with salt and vanilla extract until soft mounds form. Add sugar slowly, beating well after each addition. Add cooled cornstarch mixture. Continue beating until meringue stands in stiff peaks.

*Doris Smith*

# Pumpkin Pecan Pie

2 eggs
1/2 cup brown sugar
1/2 cup sugar
1 cup evaporated milk
2 cups 1 16 oz. can
   pumpkin
1 unbaked pie shell

1 tsp. cinnamon
1/8 tsp. ginger
1/4 tsp. allspice
1 Tbsp. flour
6 Tbsp. chopped
   pecans

Beat eggs and sugars; add pumpkin, then milk gradually. Mix flour and spices; add to pumpkin mixture. Mix well and pour into pie shell. Sprinkle pecans on top. Bake at 450 degrees for 10 minutes; reduce heat to 325 degrees and bake another 40 minutes.

*Sarah Campbell*

# Sugar Frosted Apple Pie

1 double crusted
   unbaked pie shell
6 medium apples,
   peeled and sliced
   thin
1 cup sugar or light
   brown sugar
2 1/2 Tbsp. flour

2 Tbsp. of margarine
3/4 tsp. cinnamon
1/4 tsp. nutmeg
1/4 tsp. mace
TOPPING:
1 Tbsp. sugar
1/8 tsp. nutmeg
1/8 tsp. mace

Prepare pastry. Place one half in pie pan. Mix sugar, flour and spices; add to apples and toss. Put into pie shell; dot with margarine. Cover with second pie shell. Pinch edges together, turn up and pinch again to form a stand-up edge. Flute with fork or fingers. Sprinkle top with sugar and spices. Slit top. Bake at 425 degrees for 35 minutes or until golden juices bubble through slits.

*Sarah Campbell*

# Brownie Pudding

| 1 cup flour | 1 tsp. vanilla |
| 2 tsp. baking powder | 2 Tbsp. margarine, |
| 1/2 tsp. salt | melted |
| 3/4 cup sugar | 3/4 cup chopped |
| 2 Tbsp. cocoa | pecans |
| 3/4 cup milk | |

Sift together flour, baking powder, salt, sugar, and cocoa. Add milk, vanilla, and melted margarine. Mix until smooth. Add nut meats. Pour into 8"x8" square pan.

| TOPPING: | |
| 3/4 cup brown sugar | 2 Tbsp. cocoa |
| | 1 3/4 cup hot water |

Mix brown sugar and cocoa. Sprinkle over batter. Pour hot water over entire batter. Bake at 350 degrees about 45 minutes. Serves 6 to 8.

*Kathleen Bridges*

# Chocolate Mousse Updated

| 6 oz. pkg. chocolate | 3 Tbsp. hot strong |
| bits | coffee |
| 3/4 cup scalded milk | 2 Tbsp. cointreau or |
| 2 whole eggs | dark rum |

In blender combine above ingredients.
Blend mixture at high speed for 1 1/2 minutes, pour into six ramekins and chill in refrigerator for 3 hours. Top with an almond or walnut half before serving. Serves 4-6.

*Trudy Harris*

# Caramel Rice Custard

*(A Rich Dessert That Is Inexpensive)*

**¹/₂ cup raw (short grain) regular white rice**
**5 cups milk (skim or 1% can be used)**
**3 eggs (or 5 egg whites)**
**³/₄ cup sugar**
**1 tsp. salt**
**2 tsp. vanilla extract**
**CARAMEL SYRUP:**
**¹/₂ cup sugar**

Day before or hours before serving, in top of double boiler combine rice and 4 cups milk. Cook over boiling water, stirring occasionally for 45 minutes until rice is tender. Remove from hot water. Let Cool slightly, about 10 minutes. Preheat oven to 350 degrees. Lightly butter a 2 quart soufflé dish or casserole. Place in shallow baking pan. In large bowl with wire whisk, beat eggs with remaining 1 cup milk. Add ³/₄ cup sugar, salt, and vanilla then mix well. Gradually stir in hot rice. Pour into prepared dish. Place dish into larger pan and pour hot water to 1 inch depth around soufflé dish. Bake uncovered 50 to 60 minutes or until knife inserted in custard 1 inch from edge comes out clean.

Remove soufflé dish from hot water to wire rack. Cool at room temperature 1 hour. Then refrigerate, covered with plastic wrap, until very well chilled. About 1 hour before serving, make caramel syrup. Sprinkle ¹/₂ cup sugar evenly over the bottom of a small, heavy skillet. Cook slowly over very low heat, stirring occasionally with wooden spoon, just until sugar melts and turns golden. Remove from heat, and cool slightly. Using a teaspoon, drizzle syrup over top of custard crisscross for pattern. Refrigerate until serving. Can be served with whipped cream or is good just plain.

*Doris Smith*

# Cranberry Mousse

1 cup cranberry juice
1 3 oz. pkg. raspberry flavored gelatin
1 16 oz. can whole berry cranberry sauce
1 cup heavy cream whipped

In a saucepan, heat cranberry juice to boiling. Stir in raspberry gelatin until dissolved. Stir in cranberry sauce. Chill until mixture is thickened. Fold in whipped cream and pour into serving dishes. Chill until firm. Garnish with additional whipped cream.

Makes 6-8 servings.

*Sandi Smallwood*

# Cream Puffs

1 cup water
1/2 cup butter
1 cup flour
3 eggs, well beaten
Whipped cream

Put the water in a saucepan to boil. When boiling, add butter and stir in the flour. Let cool. When cold, add the eggs. Beat all thoroughly and drop on to buttered tins. Bake 20 minutes at 400 degrees. When cool, slit with a sharp knife and fill with whipped cream.

*Marcella Miller*

# Texas Mud Squares

1 cup flour
1/2 cup butter, melted
1/2 cup chopped pecans
TOPPING:
1 3 oz. pkg. cream cheese
1 cup powdered sugar
1 cup whipped topping
2 3 oz. pkgs. chocolate pudding
2 1/2 cups milk
1 cup whipped topping
1/2 cup chopped pecans

Mix flour, butter and pecans. Pat into 13"x9"x2" pan and bake for 15 minutes at 350 degrees. Mix cream cheese and powdered sugar. Fold in 1 cup whipped topping. Spread over cooled crust. Cook pudding with milk until thick. Cool and place on other layers. Cover with whipped topping and chopped nuts. Chill and serve.

*Jeannine Miller*

# Crème Brulée

| | |
|---|---|
| ¹/₂ pt. whipping cream | 2 Tbsp. sugar |
| ¹/₂ pt. half and half | 1 Tbsp. vanilla |
| 4 egg yolks | |

Combine cream and heat until lukewarm. Whip egg yolks with sugar and add to cream. Whisk in vanilla. Pour into ramekins and place into bain marie. Bake at 325 degrees for 45 minutes. Cool to room temperature. Sprinkle with brown sugar. Put under broiler until sugar is melted. Doubles or triples well.

*Mary Stuart Lundy*

# Crème Fraiche

| | |
|---|---|
| ¹/₂ cup sour cream | 1 cup heavy cream or whipping cream |

In glass bowl mix creams. Let stand covered without disturbing in a warm place for 24 hours. Stir briskly and refrigerate at least 24 hours before serving. Serve over cold berries. This will keep up to ten days in the refrigerator. An easy but elegant topping for cold berries.

*Ruth Russell*

# Flan

| | |
|---|---|
| 1 cup sugar | 5 eggs, beaten |
| 1 qt. milk | 1 tsp. vanilla |

Melt ¹/₄ cup sugar in a small iron skillet over very low heat. Immediately pour melted sugar into a 1¹/₂ qt. mold.

Pour milk into saucepan. Add eggs and ³/₄ cup sugar to milk. Heat but do not boil. Stir well and add vanilla. Strain mixture into mold. Place mold in water bath and place in preheated 350 degree oven. Cook one hour. Refrigerate overnight. Unmold. Enjoyment for 6 to 8.

*Catherine Joseffy*

# Microwave Banana Pudding

| | |
|---|---|
| 1 cup sugar | Pinch of salt |
| 1/3 cup flour | 1/2 tsp. vanilla |
| 2 cups milk | Vanilla wafers |
| 1/2 stick margarine | 3 bananas, sliced |
| 2 eggs | |

In a two quart microwave safe bowl mix sugar, flour and salt. Add milk and blend. Microwave on high for 3 minutes. Stir well. Microwave 2 minutes more. Remove and stir small amount of pudding over beaten eggs. Blend into pudding. Microwave again until thick as desired. About 1-3 minutes. Remove and mix well with a whisk. Add vanilla to taste. Layer vanilla wafers, sliced bananas and pudding.

*Gloria Glass*

# Mother's Nice Lemon Dessert

| | |
|---|---|
| 1 cup sugar | 3 Tbsp. lemon juice, |
| 4 Tbsp. flour | plus rind |
| 1/4 tsp. salt | 1 cup milk |
| 1 Tbsp. butter or | 2 eggs |
| margarine | |

Mix sugar, flour and salt. Grate rind of half of a lemon and add along with lemon juice. Beat the egg yolks, milk and butter together and add to first mixture. Beat the egg whites until stiff and fold in. Pour into oven-proof bowl, place bowl in pan of hot water (so the water comes up 1 1/2" on sides). Bake at 325 degrees about 50 minutes. It is done when you insert knife around sides and no liquid is left.

*Betty Ethel*

# Gillespie County Fair Blue Ribbon Fudge

**12 oz. pkg. Nestle's semi-sweet chocolate chips**
**1 tsp. vanilla**
**1/2 cup butter melted**
**10 large marshmallows**
**1 5.33 oz. can evaporated milk**
**2 cups sugar**
**1 cup chopped walnuts**

In a mixer bowl, combine chocolate chips, vanilla, and melted butter. Set aside. In a heavy pan slowly melt marshmallows, milk, and sugar. After they are all melted together, turn up heat to medium and bring to a bubbly simmer, stirring constantly. Begin timing at this point; lower heat and keep at a bubbly simmer for exactly six minutes. Continue to stir constantly. It scorches very easily. Pour this mixture over the chocolate mixture in the mixing bowl. Turn mixer to stir speed and stir for about 2 minutes until batter is well mixed and looks thick. Add walnuts and mix. Pour onto waxed paper lined 9"x9" pan. Cool overnight. Yields 80 one inch squares.

*Velna Jackson*

# Rocky Road Candy

**1 pkg. large marshmallows**
**1 lb. milk chocolate**
**1 cup walnuts or other nuts of your choice**
**1 Tbsp. vegetable oil**

Butter 8"x8"x2" glass baking dish.

Cut marshmallows in quarters. In top of double boiler combine chocolate, broken into chunks, and vegetable oil. Melt over hot (not boiling) water stirring frequently. Using 1/3 to 1/2 to mixture, pour thin layer of chocolate into dish. Sprinkle with marshmallow and nuts, gently press into chocolate. Pour remaining chocolate on top. Smooth with spoon. Refrigerate until firm. Makes 36 pieces.

*Pat Reese*

# Microwave Pecan Brittle

1 cup pecan pieces
1 cup sugar
1/2 cup light corn
    syrup
1 Tbsp. margarine
1 tsp. vanilla
1 tsp. baking soda
1/8 tsp. salt

Line cookie sheet with foil and butter foil.

Combine in a glass bowl: pecans, sugar, syrup, and salt. Microwave on High 4 minutes. Stir. Microwave on High 3-4 minutes. Stir in margarine and vanilla. Microwave on High 1 minute. Stir in soda. Pour on cookie sheet immediately.

*Pat Reese*

# Microwave Toffee

1/2 cup pecans, finely
    chopped
3/4 cup chocolate
    chips
1 cup sugar
butter
1/4 cup pecans,
    chopped
1/4 cup water
1/2 cup margarine or
1 tsp. salt

Sprinkle pecans in a 9" circle on a greased cookie sheet. Coat the top 2" of a 2 1/2 qt. glass bowl with margarine; place remaining margarine in bowl. Add sugar, salt, and water. Microwave at high for 11 minutes or until mixture turns light brown; pour over pecans. Sprinkle with 1/2 cup chocolate chips. Let stand 1 minute, then sprinkle 1/4 cup chocolate chips over. Chill until chocolate is firm (takes 1 to 2 hours). Break into pieces.

*Sarah Campbell*

*FREDERICKSBURG COUNTY SEAT*                    1988
From the collection of
Karl and Judy Koch, Fredericksburg, Texas

Lee developed his unique stylized approach to painting after moving to Fredericksburg. We find in this painting a typical example of his gift for capturing the flavor of the peaceful town of Fredericksburg.

# Basic Meat Balls

2 lbs. ground lean beef
1 1/2 cups bread crumbs (takes about 3 slices bread)
1/2 cup finely chopped onions
1/2 cup finely chopped celery
1 Tbsp. worcestershire sauce
2 egg whites
2 tsp. garlic salt
1/4 tsp. fresh ground pepper

Mix ingredients together. Shape 2 dozen 1 1/2" balls. Bake in 375 degree oven for 20 minutes. Serve with desired sauce and freeze the rest. Suggested sauces: Oriental, Burgundy mushroom, Italian tomato, barbeque. Makes 2 dozen.

*Mary Hatchette*

# Black Bean And Roasted Corn Salad

4 cups black beans
1 1/2 cups fresh corn kernels
1 red bell pepper, seeds and membranes removed, diced
1 red onion, finely diced
3 stalks celery, trimmed and finely diced
1 cup soy sauce
1 cup balsamic vinegar
1 cup firmly packed coriander leaves, finely chopped
2 Tbsp. fresh marjoram, finely chopped

Fill a large pan with cold water. Soak the black beans for 1 hour, then bring the water to a boil and cook just until the beans are tender but not mushy. Drain in a colander, rinse, and let cool.

Cut the corn off the cob and place in a large cast iron pan or sauté pan. Cook over high heat until the kernels begin to pop and blacken. Remove from the heat and let cool. Add all the ingredients together in a large mixing bowl and toss thoroughly. Yield: 10 servings.

*Mary Lindsey*

## Bonnie's Bean And Barley Soup

2 cups cooked Great
  Northern beans
1 cup barley
1 cup onion, finely
  chopped
4 to 6 cloves garlic,
  chopped
1 carrot, finely
  chopped

1 stalk celery, finely
  chopped
1/3 cup brown rice
miso (found in
  health food stores)
1 tsp. lemon/black
  pepper seasoning
1 tsp. no-salt garlic
  and herb seasoning

Cook barley in $3^1/2$ cups of water for 1 hour and 15 minutes. Combine $1^1/2$ cups water, onion, garlic, carrot, celery, miso, and remaining spices. Simmer 10 minutes over low heat. Add cooked beans and barley. Add bean liquid and water for desired consistency. Heat thoroughly and serve. Yield: 6 servings

*Bonnie Greene*

## Carrot And Raisin Cake

2 cups grated carrots
$1^1/2$ cups sugar
$1^1/3$ cups water
2 cups raisins

$1/2$ tsp. each salt,
  cinnamon, cloves,
  nutmeg and
  allspice
2 cups flour
1 cup chopped nuts
1 tsp. baking soda

Boil first four ingredients plus spices and salt together for 5 minutes. Cool well. Add flour, nuts and baking soda. Put in loaf pan or mini loaf pans and bake at 300 degrees one hour or longer until firm, or reduce oven temperature to 200 degrees and bake 15 to 20 minutes longer.

*Mary Lou White*

# Cherry Tomatoes

2 cups cherry
   tomatoes, fresh
2 Tbsp. olive oil
2 tsp. shallots,
   chopped

2 tsp. scallions,
   chopped
1 tsp. dillweed
$^1/_4$ tsp. parsley,
   chopped

Sauté all ingredients in heavy skillet. Add tomatoes and cook up to bursting point. Make sure tomatoes are covered in sauce. Serve immediately. Serves 6.

*Lauren Bade*

# Low Fat Salad Dressing

$^2/_3$ cup Rice Vinegar
$^1/_3$ cup Safflower oil
3 tsp. country style
   mustard

$^1/_2$ tsp. garlic powder
2 tsp. lemon juice
White pepper
4 pkgs. Equal

Mix all ingredients well. 1 teaspoon = 30 calories.

*Lauren Bade*

# Chicken Dinner In The Pot

*A very good one-pot dinner. Children like it, too.*

2 chicken breasts,
   split and skinned
4 medium-size
   potatoes
2 large carrots
$^1/_2$ lb. fresh green
   beans, or 1 10 oz.
   pkg. frozen

1 large onion
1 Tbsp. dried parsley
   flakes
Salt and pepper
$^1/_2$ cup dry sherry

Preheat oven to 300 degrees. Place chicken breasts in a large, heavy ovenware pot. (An enamel-coated cast-iron pot is best.) Peel potatoes, slice $^1/_2$ inch thick and place on top of chicken. Peel and quarter the onion. Peel carrots, quarter lengthwise, and cut into 2 inch lengths. Cut ends off the green beans, or separate frozen beans, and place in the pot with onions and carrots. Sprinkle contents of pot with parsley flakes. Season lightly with salt and pepper. Pour sherry over all and cover tightly. Bake 2 hours, or until vegetables are tender. Yield: 4 servings

*Lauren Bade*

# Fat Free Pumpkin Raisin Cake

1²/₃ cups flour
²/₃ cup sugar
¼ cup non-fat dry milk
1 tsp. baking soda
½ tsp. baking powder
½ tsp. salt
2 tsps. pumpkin pie spice
½ cup raisins
2 egg whites
1 cup canned solid-pack pumpkin
¹/₃ cup white corn syrup
¹/₃ cup orange juice

Spray 9" square baking pan with cooking spray. In large bowl combine dry ingredients and raisins. In medium bowl combine remaining ingredients. Add to dry ingredients; stir until smooth. Pour into prepared pan. Bake in 350 degree oven 35 minutes. Cool in pan on wire rack.

*Doris Smith*

# Foil Fish Bake

½ cup chopped dill sprigs
4 fresh lake trout, or any white fish (2 lbs. in all)
¼ cup chopped chives
¼ cup chopped onion
½ cup chopped parsley
2 Tbsp. margarine
2 Tbsp. lemon juice

Preheat oven to 400 degrees. Clean and rinse fish; allow to drain. Sprinkle lightly with salt. Make stuffing: Mix together margarine, parsley, dill sprigs, chives, onion, and lemon juice. Stuff and wrap each fish separately in aluminum foil, sealing the edges carefully. Bake 20 minutes. Unwrap, remove to a hot platter, garnish with parsley and lemon slices. Yield: 4 servings

*Effie Hinkelstein*

# Herbed Quesadillas

¹/₂ onion, peeled and cut in ¹/₄" slices, quarter the slices

¹/₄ cup white wine or water

8 8" flour tortillas

1 red bell pepper or medium sized jar minced pimiento, drained

¹/₂ lb. grated low fat mozzarella cheese

2 garlic cloves, peeled and minced

2 Tbsp. chopped fresh marjoram or 1 tsp. dried

2 Tbsp. chopped fresh oregano or 1 tsp. dried

Fresh ground pepper

Steam-sauté onion and garlic until softened slightly. To peel red pepper, cut in half and broil until skin starts to turn black. Plunge into ice water and let cool a few minutes. Rub the skin to loosen it and peel skin off. Cut peeled pepper into inch long strips about ¹/₄" wide. Mix together cooked onions, garlic, pepper, cheese, and spices. Divide evenly over 4 tortillas and top with remaining flour tortillas. Press down gently. At this point they may be covered tightly with foil and refrigerated for a day or so.

To cook, preheat oven to 400 degrees. Place quesadillas on cookie sheet, cover lightly with foil and bake about 8 minutes or until cheese is melted. Cut into quarters and serve. Picante dipping sauce on the side is good. Makes 16 pieces.

*Mary Hatchette*

# Joe Stiver's Hawaiian Chicken

- 4 cut up chickens, cut into 4 pieces (2 legs, 2 thighs, 2 breasts, no backs)
- 3 cloves garlic, crushed
- 1 piece of ginger
- 2 lemons, juiced
- 1 jigger of rum or bourbon

MARINADE:
- 3 cups soy sauce
- 3 Tbsp. white sugar

Marinate the chicken the day before you cook. Put chicken and marinade into baking dish. Cover with foil. Cook 45 minutes at 325 degrees. Take foil off. Cook 1 more hour, basting with marinade.

Serve with browned coconut. Serves 12

*Lauren Bade*

# Key Lime Pie

- 1 8 oz. pkg. Healthy Choice Cream Cheese, softened
- 1 cup graham cracker crumbs
- 3 Tbsp. melted low-fat margarine
- 2 Tbsp. NutraSweet
- 1 1/4 oz. envelope unflavored gelatin (Knox)
- 1 3/4 cups skim milk
- 1/3 to 1/2 cup lime juice
- 1/2 cup NutraSweet Spoonful
- Lime slices
- Mint sprigs

Combine graham crackers, margarine and 2 Tbsp. NutraSweet in bottom of 7" springform pan; pat evenly on sides and 1/2 inch up the side of the pan.

Sprinkle gelatin over 1/2 cup of the milk in a small saucepan; let stand 2 to 3 minutes. Cook over low heat, stirring constantly, until gelatin is dissolved. Beat cream cheese until fluffy in a small bowl; beat in remaining 1 1/4 cup milk and the gelatin mixture. Mix in lime juice and 1/2 cup NutraSweet. Refrigerate until set, about 2 hours. This pie is quite tart and minimally sweet.

*NANA'S TEA ROOM, Fredericksburg*

# Lemon-Baked Chicken

*A touch of lemon gives this
golden baked chicken a delicate flavor.*

1 frying chicken (2¹/₂-
3 pounds), cut into
serving pieces
2 Tbsp. oil or melted
margarine

3 Tbsp. fresh lemon
juice
1 clove garlic, crushed
¹/₂ tsp. salt
Dash pepper

Preheat oven to 350 degrees. In a bowl combine lemon juice, oil, garlic, salt, and pepper. Arrange chicken in a shallow casserole or baking pan and pour over it the lemon and oil mixture. Cover and bake until tender, about 40 minutes, basting occasionally. Uncover casserole and bake 10 minutes longer to allow chicken to brown. To serve, sprinkle with chopped parsley. Yield: 4 servings

*Virginia Muncey*

# Melenzana Alla Griglia (Broiled Eggplant)

1 large eggplant
¹/₂ cup Italian salad
dressing
1 tsp. rosemary
¹/₄ tsp. oregano

1 cup tomato sauce
Salt and pepper
2 oz. grated parmesan
cheese

Peel eggplant and cut crosswise in ³/₄ inch slices. Place in a bowl with salad dressing, rosemary and oregano, being certain dressing and herbs are spread over each eggplant slice. Let stand 1 hour. Drain. Arrange eggplant slices on a baking sheet. Broil 3 inches from a medium-low flame about 5 minutes on each side until the slices are tender and lightly browned. Arrange the eggplant and tomato sauce in alternate layers in an 8 inch square baking dish, seasoning each layer lightly with salt and pepper. Top with grated cheese. Place under broiler again for about 2 minutes or until cheese is brown. Serve immediately. Yield: 6 servings

*Evelyn Samuels*

# Moroccan Eggplant Salad

**2 medium eggplants**

**1 small onion, chopped**

**3 cloves garlic, finely minced**

**1 Tbsp. ground cumin**

**2 tsp. paprika**

**1/2 tsp. or less cayenne pepper**

**1/4 cup fresh lemon juice (or to taste)**

**1 Tbsp. olive oil**

**1/4 cup plain, nonfat yogurt**

**3 large ripe tomatoes, peeled if desired, diced into 1/2" pieces**

**1/4 cup freshly chopped parsley**

**Salt and freshly ground black pepper to taste**

**Roasted red-pepper strips**

Preheat the oven to 450 degrees. Prick each eggplant in a few places with a fork. Roast on a baking sheet until tender but not mushy, about 45 minutes. Let stand until cool enough to handle, then peel and cut into 1 1/2" cubes. Drain in a colander, then transfer to a large bowl.

Place onion, garlic, spices and lemon juice in a food processor or blender; process until completely liquefied. Pour over the eggplant.

Add olive oil, yogurt, tomatoes and parsley; mix gently with your hands so that the eggplant doesn't break down. Season to taste with salt and pepper, and add more lemon juice and spices if needed. Arrange red-pepper strips on top. Yield: 6 to 8 servings

*Virginia Kahler*

# No-Fat Mocha Cake

1 cup flour
1/3 cup plus 2 Tbsp.
  cocoa powder
1 tsp. instant espresso
  powder or instant
  coffee powder
1 tsp. baking powder
1 tsp. baking soda
6 large egg whites,
  room temperature

1 1/3 cups packed
  brown sugar
1 cup coffee-flavored
  non-fat yogurt
1 tsp. vanilla
1 Tbsp. powdered
  sugar
1/2 tsp. cinnamon

Preheat oven to 350 degrees. Line bottom of 9" cake pan with waxed paper. Spray with vegetable oil spray. Dust with flour. Sift into medium bowl flour, 1/3 cup plus 1 Tbsp. cocoa, espresso powder, baking powder and soda. In mixer beat egg whites, brown sugar, yogurt and vanilla about 1 minute. Add dry ingredients. Transfer to pan and bake until tester comes out clean, about 35 minutes. Cool in pan on rack 15 minutes. Turn out and cool completely. Combine remaining 1 Tbsp. cocoa, powdered sugar and cinnamon and sift over cake.

*Linda Zehnder*

# Oven French Fries

*French fries without frying — a surprise for those who thought this crispy treat was a forbidden food.*

4 medium potatoes
  (Irish potatoes are
  good)

1 Tbsp. oil

Preheat oven to 475 degrees. Peel potatoes and cut into long strips about 1/2 inch wide. Dry strips thoroughly on paper towels. Toss in a bowl with oil. When strips are thoroughly coated with the oil, spread them in a single layer on a cookie sheet and place in preheated oven for 35 minutes. Turn strips periodically to brown on all sides. If a crispier, browner potato is desired, run under broiler for a minute or two. Sprinkle with salt before serving. Yield: 6 servings. 80 calories.

*Kristi Miller*

# Persian-Style Chicken Brochette

**1 large onion, cut into
chunks (about 1 1/2
cups)**

**1/2 cup fresh lemon
juice**

**2 tsp. finely minced
garlic**

**2 Tbsp. dried oregano**

**2 Tbsp. olive oil**

**1 cup white wine**

**6 boneless, skinless
chicken breast
halves, trimmed of
excess fat, cut in 2"
cubes**

**Salt and freshly
ground black
pepper to taste**

**1 Tbsp. paprika**

To make marinade, puree onion, lemon juice, paprika, garlic, and oregano together in a blender or food processor. Stir in olive oil and wine.

Place chicken in a nonaluminum container. Pour marinade over chicken and toss well to coat. Cover and refrigerate at least 6 hours or overnight. Bring the chicken to room temperature. Heat a grill or broiler. Remove chicken from the marinade and thread on each of 6 skewers; sprinkle with salt and pepper. Grill or broil chicken away from flame, about 2 minutes on each side. Serve with rice and lemon wedges. Yield: 6 servings/236 calories.

*Virginia Kahler*

# Phyllo Egg Rolls

2 celery stalks
$1/2$ medium onion
8 snow peas
4 Tbsp. red or green
    bell pepper
$1^1/2$ cup green cabbage
4 stalks bok choy
    cabbage
$1/2$ cup bean sprouts
2 Tbsp. reduced
    sodium soy sauce
2 tsp. rice wine
    vinegar

1 Tbsp. sherry
$1/2$ tsp. cayenne
    pepper
$1/2$ tsp. ground
    coriander
$1/4$ cup chopped
    cilantro or parsley
2 tsp. grated ginger
1 tsp. fresh minced
    garlic
1 tsp. sesame oil

Cut celery, onion, bell pepper, cabbages into julienne slices. Mix and stir fry with sesame oil all other ingredients in large skillet or wok for a few minutes.

Preheat oven to 375 degrees. Separate a sheet of phyllo. Cover remaining sheets with damp towel. Fold phyllo sheet to make a 9"x14" rectangle. Place $1/2$ cup of vegetable filling in lower center of the 14" side; shape filling into about a 4" rectangle. Fold in the sides of phyllo dough and roll it up to shape the egg roll. Place on lightly oiled baking pan seam side down. (Making the egg rolls is easier to do than it is to describe!) Don't worry if the phyllo dough tears a little. Make the rest of the rolls.

Spray or brush rolls lightly with vegetable oil and bake 10-12 minutes until rolls are golden brown. Serve with appropriate sauces. Shrimp, chicken, or pork can be added if desired. Leftover rolls can be frozen.

*Mary Hatchette*

# Turkey Soup

| | |
|---|---|
| 1 | onion, chopped |
| 1 | carrot, chopped |
| 1 | stalk of celery, chopped |
| 2 Tbsp. | unsalted butter |
| 1/4 cup | flour |
| 4 cups | chicken stock |
| 1 cup | dry white wine |
| 1 | turkey carcass |
| 2 sprigs | parsley |
| 1/2 tsp. | dry thyme |
| 1 | bay leaf |
| 6 | peppercorns |

Sauté onions, carrot, and celery in butter stirring for 7 to 10 minutes or until golden. Add flour, stirring for 2 minutes. Stir in stock, 4 cups of water, and wine. Bring to a boil. Add turkey carcass, parsley, thyme, bay leaf, and peppercorns. Simmer soup. Skim and cook 1 1/2 hours.

*Ruby del Rio*

# Vegetarian Spaghetti Sauce

| | |
|---|---|
| 1 | medium onion, finely chopped |
| 4 to 5 | cloves of garlic, finely chopped |
| 3/4 cup | white wine |
| 1 28 oz. can | whole tomatoes, chopped |
| 2 | medium tomatoes, chopped |
| 1 | medium zucchini, finely chopped |
| 1/4 cup | parsley, chopped |
| 1 tsp. | oregano |
| 1/2 tsp. | thyme |
| 1/2 tsp. | basil |

Sauté onions and garlic in wine until transparent. Add remaining ingredients and simmer over low heat until zucchini is tender but not mushy. Serve over pasta or a combination of brown and wild rice. Yield: 4 servings.

*Bonnie Green*

# Lemony Sponge Pudding

2 Tbsps. regular (not calorie reduced) margarine

³/₄ cup granulated sugar, divided

2 eggs, separated, at room temperature

5 Tbsp. fresh lemon juice

Dash of salt

3 Tbsp. flour

1 cup plus 2 Tbsp. low-fat milk

2 tsp. finely grated lemon peel

Lemon slices and mint sprigs

Preheat oven to 350 degrees. Coat 1¹/₂ quart baking dish or six custard cups lightly with nonstick cooking spray. In mixer bowl cream margarine and ¹/₂ cup of the sugar until smooth. Add egg yolks, one at a time, beating well after each addition, until mixture is thick. Beat in flour, alternating with milk, peel and lemon juice, in two additions. Set aside. In another bowl, using clean beaters, beat egg whites on medium high speed until foamy. Sprinkle in salt and continue beating until soft peaks form. Beat in remaining ¹/₄ cup sugar, 1 tablespoon at a time, until whites form stiff peaks. Lightly fold whites into yolk mixture. Spoon into baking dish or cups and place in large pan filled with 1 inch hot water. Bake until custard is puffed and lightly browned (45 minutes in baking dish, 35 minutes in individual cups). Remove from water and cool on wire rack. Serve warm or chilled, garnish with lemon slices and mint springs.

Nutrients per serving: calories 138, protein 4g, carbohydrates 31g, fat 7g, cholesterol 96mg, sodium 127mg.

*Nancy O'Neal*

# Cream of Broccoli Soup

³/₄ cup minced onion
1 clove garlic, minced
1 Tbsp. olive oil
1 Tbsp. flour
1¹/₄ cups defatted
chicken broth
2 cups fresh broccoli
stems

¹/₄ tsp. ground thyme
Fresh ground black
pepper to taste
Steam broccoli stems
1 cup skimmed milk

Steam broccoli stems
(save florets for
other use) until
tender

In a 2 qt. pot, sauté onions and garlic in olive oil until soft. Add flour, cook, stirring constantly about 1 minute. Add broth a little at a time. Stir until smooth. Add broccoli, thyme, and pepper. Bring to boil, simmer uncovered 5 minutes. Add milk and simmer uncovered 5 minutes. Purée in blender a small amount at a time until all is smooth. Can be made ahead of time and refrigerated. Heat before serving.

Optional: garnish with fresh parsley or a thin slice of lemon. For spicier soup, add a few drops of hot sauce or red pepper flakes. Makes about one quart.

*Pat Kreuz*

LEE ETHEL

*TWO TEN WEST TRAVIS*                                    1987

From the collection of
Bob and Janice Phelps, New Orleans, Louisiana

This painting was commissioned by Bob Phelps to include the home of his mother (Ellison Phelps). The home is the yellow house in the upper right hand corner.

The upper left portion of the painting was chosen for the cover of the book. The St. Barnabas Chapel appears in the foreground.

# Addie's Salad Dressing

4 Tbsp. parsley
2 shallots (or small white onion)
1 tsp. dry mustard
1 tsp. Hungarian paprika
1 tsp. salt
6 Tbsp. honey
6 Tbsp. cider vinegar
2 Tbsp. fresh lemon juice
2/3 cup light oil (Mazola or Wesson)

Process onion and parsley in food processor. Add rest of ingredients and process until well blended.

*Anne Weigers*

# Bar-B-Q Sauce

1 20 oz. bottle catsup
1 1/2 cups brown sugar
5 Tbsp. liquid smoke
1 tsp. tabasco
1 tsp. worcestershire sauce
1 Tbsp. mustard

Combine all ingredients and simmer about 10 minutes.

# Coffee Ice Cream Punch

1 gallon strong coffee, allow to cool
1/2 gallon coffee ice cream
1 pint vanilla ice cream
1 pint heavy cream, whipped
Nutmeg or cinnamon

Blend coffee and half of the coffee ice cream to a fairly thick consistency. Chill in a punch bowl in refrigerator. When ready to serve, mix in ice cream balls made with the remaining quart of coffee ice cream and the vanilla ice cream. Top with heaps of whipped cream. Sprinkle with nutmeg or cinnamon. A refreshing change from coffee or tea for warm weather entertaining. Makes about 20-30 cups.

*Lady Bird Johnson*

# Court Bouillon

*(For Poaching Or Base For Sauces)*

| | |
|---|---|
| 1 qt. water | 1/4 cup chopped parsley |
| 1/2 tsp. salt | 1 pinch of thyme |
| 10 oz. white wine or lemon juice | 4 pepper corns |
| 1/2 cup chopped onion | 1 bayleaf |
| 1/2 cup chopped celery | 1 clove |
| 1/2 cup chopped carrots | |

Boil for full minute, strain and store in refrigerator.

*Alethia Alt*

# Dilled Okra Pickles

| | |
|---|---|
| 2 hot peppers (one red and one green) | 1 qt. white vinegar (undistilled) |
| 2 garlic cloves | 1 cup water |
| 2 heads fresh dill or 1 tsp. dill seed | 1/2 cup pure salt (not iodized) |

If heads of fresh dill or dill seed is used, place 1/2 teaspoon in bottom of jar and 1/2 teaspoon on top of pickles. Pack in sterilized jars fresh okra which has been washed. Pack as tightly as possible without bruising. (If you bruise them, the pickles won't be crisp.)

Bring vinegar, water, and salt to a boil and pour over okra in jars, covering completely.

Seal jars. Okra should be ready after 2 weeks. Serve icy cold. Makes 4 to 5 pints.

*Lady Bird Johnson*

# Fapy's Best Ever Salad Dressing

1 heaping Tbsp. Dijon
  mustard
1/2 cup red wine
  vinegar
2 large cloves or
  garlic, pressed
Seasoned salt
Pepper
1 cup olive oil

Combine all ingredients in a jar; shake well; enjoy!

*Cay Meadows*

# Float 'em Syrup

4 cups sugar
1 cup water
2 cups boiling water
1 cup corn syrup
1/2 tsp. maple
  flavoring
1/4 tsp. vanilla extract

Combine the sugar and the 1 cup water. Mix well. Cook without stirring until the syrup is a light caramel color 338 degrees. Remove from heat. Very gradually stir in boiling water. Add corn syrup. Boil 2 to 3 minutes, stirring. Add flavorings. Store cooled syrup in container; cover. Yield: 5 cups syrup.

*Gretchen McWilliams*

# Fresh Tomato Sauce For Pasta

6 large ripe tomatoes,
  seeded, peeled &
  coarsely chopped
1/3 cup olive oil
2 cloves garlic,
  crushed
1 large onion, chopped
1/2 cup chopped
  parsley
1/2 cup fresh basil
Salt & fresh ground
  pepper
Few drops of Tabasco

Sauté garlic and onion in olive oil until onion is limp (about 10 minutes). Add everything else, stir well, cover and simmer for 10-15 minutes. Serve over freshly cooked hot pasta. Sprinkle with additional chopped parsley and parmesan cheese.

*Anne Weigers*

# Fruit Drink

1 cup ripe strawberries
1 ripe banana
1 cup orange juice
1/2 cup cracked ice

Beat in electric blender until smooth.

*Lindsey Straka*

# Green Mango Chutney

3 lbs. green mango, chopped
1 can pineapple tidbits
1 lb. seedless raisins, chopped
1 lb. currants
1/2 lb. cashews, chopped
2 lb. raw sugar
1 qt. cider vinegar
1 head garlic, chopped fine

3 1/2 to 7 oz. jar jalapeño, chopped (fresh if desired)
1 1 oz. can mustard seed
1 tsp. salt
1/2 tsp. pepper
1/2 tsp. cinnamon
1/2 tsp. ground clove
1/2 tsp. celery salt
Rind of 1 orange, grated

Boil until thick, about 1 hour. Pour into sterile glass jars and seal tightly. Makes 8 to 9 pints. GOOD!

*Mary Lindsey*

# Horseradish Mousse For Beef

1 3 oz. pkg. of lemon jello
1 cup of boiling water
1/4 tsp. salt
1 Tbsp. vinegar
1 cup sour cream
1/4 cup horseradish
1 tsp. finely chopped onion (optional)

Dissolve and let set. Whip together and pour in greased mold. Make a day ahead for better flavor. Unmold and serve with steaks, beef roast, etc.

*Gretchen McWilliams*

# Hot Buttered Rum

1 lb. butter, softened
1 lb. light brown sugar
1 lb. powdered sugar
2 tsp. ground cinnamon
2 tsp. ground nutmeg
1 qt. vanilla ice cream
1 oz. rum per drink

Combine all above except ice cream beat until light and fluffy. Add softened ice cream. Blend well.

Spoon mixture into 2 quart freezer container and freeze.

To serve: Thaw slightly. Place 3 heaping Tbsp. of mixture into large mug. Add rum. Fill with boiling water. Stir. Serve with whipped cream and cinnamon stick.

*Jean Wilkerson Fourrier*

# Jezebel Sauce

3 oz. horseradish
1 1³/₈ oz. can dry mustard
1 18 oz. jar pineapple preserves
1 18 oz. jar apple jelly
1 Tbsp. coarse black pepper

Blend horseradish and mustard. Add remaining ingredients. Be sure all is completely blended. Refrigerate. Keeps well for months. Serve with roast, or as a dip for fried chicken. Spread over cream cheese.

*Mary Ann Smith*

# Peach Butter

**3 cups fresh or frozen peaches**
**1/4 cup orange juice**
**3/4 cup sugar**
**2 Tbsp. honey**
**1/8 tsp. ground allspice**
**1/2 tsp. grated orange rind**

Combine peaches and orange juice in a saucepan. Bring to a boil over medium heat, cover, reduce heat and simmer 5-10 minutes or until peaches are tender, stirring occasionally. Spoon into an electric blender; process peaches until smooth. Return to saucepan; add sugar and remaining ingredients and bring to a boil. Reduce heat and simmer, uncovered, 5-10 minutes or until thickened, stirring occasionally. Cool. Store in refrigerator. Serve on pancakes, biscuits or toast. Baste on chicken or pork chops.
Yield: 1 1/2 cups.

*Sande Knapp*

# Sangria

**4 liters dry red wine**
**2 6 oz. cans frozen lemonade concentrate**
**1 24 oz. club soda**
**2 oranges thinly sliced**
**2 lemons thinly sliced**
**2 limes thinly sliced**

Mix first three ingredients well. Add sliced fruit. Chill and serve.

*Elena Smith*

# Snap Crackle Popcorn

16 cups popped corn
(about $^3/_4$ cups
unpopped popcorn)
$1^1/_2$ cups pecans
$1^1/_2$ cups walnuts
1 cup packed brown
sugar

$^1/_2$ cup butter or
margarine (1 stick)
$^1/_2$ cup light corn
syrup (white karo)
$^1/_2$ tsp. salt
$^1/_2$ teaspoon vanilla
extract

Preheat oven to 250 degrees. Place popped corn, pecans, and walnuts in large open roasting pan ($17^1/_4$"x$11^1/_2$"); set aside. To prepare caramel coating; in heavy saucepan over medium heat, heat brown sugar, corn syrup and salt to boiling. Boil 5 minutes, stirring frequently. Remove saucepan from heat and stir in vanilla extract. Pour hot sugar mixture over popped corn mixture, stirring to coat well.

Bake popped corn mixture 1 hour, stirring occasionally. Spoon caramel covered popcorn into another large roasting pan or onto waxed paper to cool, stirring occasionally to separate. Store popcorn mixture in tightly covered containers. I give this out every Christmas.

*Doris Smith*

| WINES | CHEESES | MEATS | SEAFOOD | DESSERT |
|---|---|---|---|---|
| **Dry White** | | | | |
| *Chardonnay* | Brie | Escargot | Seafood (cream sauce, pan fried) | Biscotti |
| | Swiss | Veal (light sauce) | Smoked fish | |
| *Fume Blanc* | Bisques | Turkey | Oysters | |
| | Emmental | Chicken (Baked, Grilled) | Dark flesh-fish | |
| | Port Salut | Pasta (oil, garlic, or fish sauce) | Lobster | |
| *Cabernet Blanc* | Swiss | Pork Roast | Shrimp (boiled or barbequed) | |
| | Jarlsberg | Ham | Cocktail sauce | Raspberry Mousse |
| | Jack | Barbeque | River fish | |
| | Gouda | Fajitas | Salads | |
| | | Chicken (garlic or tomato) | | |
| **Semi Dry** | | | | |
| *Cabernet Blanc* | Smoked | Sweet breads | Seafood (Cajun or blackened) | Sherbet |
| | Mozzarella | Pasta (white sauce) | Shellfish | Fruit Pies |
| | Muenster | Oriental dishes | Trout | Tarts |
| | Goat Cheese | Pate | Clams | Flan |
| | (Chevre) | Lemon Sauces | | Sweet Citrus |
| | | Winged game | | |
| **Reds** | | | | |
| *Cabernet* | Cheddar | Pizza | Fish Stew | Strawberries |
| *Sauvignon* | Cheesestraws | Spicy Meats | Snails | Raspberries |
| | Gruyere | Poultry | | Pecans |
| *Cabernet Trois* | | All beef dishes | | |
| | | Pasta (red sauce) | | |
| | | Lamb, Goose and Game | | |
| | | Barbeque | | |
| **Dessert** | | | | |
| *Cabernet Blanc* | Gorgonzola | Sweetbreads | White Fish (rich sauces) | Dark Fruit |
| | Blue-vein cheeses | Veal | Fruit sauces | Pies, Tarts |
| | Gjestost | Pate | | Flan |
| | Stilton | Port Soup | | Meringue |
| | | Duck | | Ginger |
| | | | | Ice Cream |

Courtesy: GRAPE CREEK VINEYARD (Ned and Nell Simes), Stonewall, Texas

# Index

**St. Barnabas ECW Cookbook**
**601 West Creek Street**
**Fredericksburg, Texas 78624**

Please send _____ copy(ies)     @ $15.00 each _____

    Texas residents sales tax     @     1.24 each _____

    Postage and handling     @     2.00 each _____

                      Total _____

Mail to:

Name _____

Address _____

City _____

State _____Zip _____

Make checks payable to *St. Barnabas ECW Cookbook.*

**St. Barnabas ECW Cookbook**
**601 West Creek Street**
**Fredericksburg, Texas 78624**

Please send _____ copy(ies)     @ $15.00 each _____

    Texas residents sales tax     @     1.24 each _____

    Postage and handling     @     2.00 each _____

                      Total _____

Mail to:

Name _____

Address _____

City _____

State _____Zip _____

Make checks payable to *St. Barnabas ECW Cookbook.*

St. Barnabas Episcopal Church
601 West Creek Street
Fredericksburg, Texas 78624

Bless, O Lord, this food to our use, and us to thy service.